Deficiencies in the
Justification of the Ungodly

Deficiencies in the Justification of the Ungodly

A Look at N. T. Wright's View of
the Doctrine of Imputed Righteousness

MANNY ALANIZ

Foreword by
BEN D. CRAVER

WIPF & STOCK · Eugene, Oregon

DEFICIENCIES IN THE JUSTIFICATION OF THE UNGODLY
A Look at N. T. Wright's View of the Doctrine of Imputed Righteousness

Copyright © 2013 Manny Alaniz. All rights reserved. Except for brief quotations in critical publications or reviews, no part of this book may be reproduced in any manner without prior written permission from the publisher. Write: Permissions, Wipf and Stock Publishers, 199 W. 8th Ave., Suite 3, Eugene, OR 97401.

All Scripture quotations, unless otherwise indicated, are taken from the New Revised Standard Version Bible, copyright © 1989, Division of Christian Education of the National Council of the Churches of Christ in the United States of America. Used by permission. All rights reserved.

Wipf & Stock
An imprint of Wipf and Stock Publishers
199 W. 8th Ave., Suite 3
Eugene, OR 97401

www.wipfandstock.com

ISBN 13: 978-1-62032-888-0

Manufactured in the U.S.A.

To my beloved wife, Sandy

You are the love of my life and the person who is most dear to my heart. The ministry journey we undertook together several years ago has truly been a walk of faith. Although it has been difficult at times, the Lord has showered us with His loving kindness. We have only begun to taste the sweetness of His glory. Thank you for your loving support, encouragement and fellowship. You truly are the bride of my youth.

Tu Solo Tu

Contents

Foreword by Ben D. Craver / ix
Preface / xi

Introduction / 1

1 An Excursus into the New Perspective on Paul / 9
2 N. T. Wright / 29
3 The Traditional View of Imputed Righteousness / 46
4 Critical Evaluation / 70

Conclusion / 93

Bibliography / 95

Foreword

N. T. WRIGHT IS one of the best-known and most respected New Testament scholars in the world. He has written over thirty books, both at the scholarly level and for popular reading. His popularity with the masses does not mean, however, that he is free from controversy among scholars. Some ask openly, "What are we to do with N. T. Wright?," fearing that he is leading his readers into error, especially regarding the doctrine of justification by faith. Wright's enthusiasm for the New Perspective on Paul (NPP) has caused another to ask, "What's wrong with Wright?"—a not-so-subtle jab at an allegedly faulty reinterpretation of the great apostle Paul, again with treacherous implications for the doctrine of justification.

It should come then as no surprise that theological students continue to be captivated by Wright. Manny Alaniz is no exception. When Manny initially contacted me about serving as his thesis supervisor, I was high and dry in the desert sky of Albuquerque, New Mexico, hundreds of miles from the semi-tropical palms and live oaks of San Antonio, Texas, where Manny was studying at Wayland Baptist University.

I had never met Manny Alaniz, did not know of his interest in Wright, and clearly had no knowledge that I was about to become a thesis advisor for the third time.

Foreword

Accepting the job has been rewarding, and a little frustrating from time to time. If Manny wants to fill you in on the frustrating parts, that will be his decision.

I must say that Manny's labor forced me to read Tom Wright in much more detail than I had previously done, an admission that is slightly embarrassing to disclose. I found Wright to be engaging and alarmingly prolific! Do not think you may have read Wright's last word on a subject; else he will publish a new tome overnight!

From the thesis came this book. It is a predictable yet enthusiastic investigation of the NPP movement and Wright's view of imputed righteousness. It indicates that the views of Krister Stendahl, E. P. Sanders, and James D. G. Dunn are foundational for understanding Wright's view of the NPP movement, which captures his view of imputed righteousness. It is also a tribute in many ways to the scholars who remain immersed in study and reflection on Wright and his thinking.

I particularly appreciated Manny's conclusion that Wright's view of imputed righteousness is deficient due to his emphasis on ecclesiology rather than soteriology. Manny argues, "The ecclesiological emphasis does not deal with the problem of guilt due to sin." Such a position diminishes the sacrificial atonement of Christ and fails to wrestle with the distinctively human problem of sin and of Divine wrath upon sin. How Wright ultimately addresses the question of God's justification of the unjust and defends his perspective on right covenant standing are concerns that the remainder of the book addresses.

I am pleased to recommend it to you!

Ben D. Craver, PhD
Associate Professor of Religion
Wayland Baptist University
San Antonio, Texas

Preface

THE LORD GOD ALMIGHTY is truly loving and merciful. He blesses humanity with an intellect whereby we as humans (although fallen), through the power of the Holy Spirit, can seek to understand his divine word. Christians throughout the centuries have agreed and disagreed with one another regarding doctrinal issues. However, the gospel prevails to this day as Christianity's core message. Justification comes from the grace of God the Father through the life and work of Jesus Christ our Lord, imputed (by God's declaration) by the power of the Holy Spirit to the ungodly.

Although the meaning of God's imputed declaration has come under fire by New Perspective on Paul (NPP) theologians such as N. T. Wright, the privilege of proclaiming the good news of grace for salvation through Christ remains the primary commission for the church. Further, the privilege of being able to debate biblical doctrines will (we pray) ultimately glorify God. The debate of biblical or theological issues revitalizes the Christian community by directing our focus to God's divine word. The words of the first two verses of Laurence Tuttiett's hymn "O Grant Us Light" ring true as Christians seek the guidance of the Holy Spirit in their study of Holy Scripture.

Preface

> O grant us light, that we may know
> The wisdom Thou alone canst give;
> That truth may guide where'er we go,
> And virtue bless where're we live!
>
> O grant us light, that we may see
> Where error lurks in human lore,
> And turn our doubting minds to Thee,
> And love Thy simple Word the more.

In the last few months, the challenges of gaining a better understanding of the NPP, particularly Wright's New Perspective view of the doctrine of imputed righteousness, have resulted in a better understanding of the traditional Protestant Reformed view of this doctrine. I now hold an even deeper and more respectful admiration for our church fathers who struggled with the doctrines of justification and imputed righteousness.

I would like to thank everyone who helped me through this process, including pastors Tom Gibbs, Victor Martinez, and Brandon Eggar. Special thanks goes out to my thesis professor, Dr. Ben Craver, for his responses, edits, patience, and words of encouragement. This thesis was one of the most difficult undertakings of my life, but in hindsight one of the most rewarding.

> Blessed are the people who know the festal shout, who walk, O Lord, in the light of your countenance; they exult in your name all day long, and in your righteousness are exalted. (Ps 89:15–16 ESV)

Introduction

"Abraham believed God, and it was reckoned [imputed] to him as righteousness" (Rom 4:3). This verse from the Apostle Paul's epistle to the Romans (cf. Gen 15:6) reveals God's mercy and glory to the ungodly by the imputation of His righteousness for Abraham who believed.[1] In Romans, Paul goes on to proclaim that the imputed righteousness spoken about in Genesis is not for Abraham alone, but for all persons saved by God through faith (Rom 4:23–24). Abraham and all who believe in the promises of God glorify God by trusting in his promises and thereby recognizing their own ungodliness.[2] So then, for the person "who without works trusts him who justifies the ungodly, such faith is reckoned as righteousness" (Rom 4:5). This is a description of the doctrine of imputed righteousness, which finds its theological clarity in the Pauline writings of Holy Scripture.[3]

---

1. Murray, *Romans*, xiii; Barrett, *Romans*, 1; Morris, *Romans*, 2. The Apostle Paul's authorship of this epistle has never been in serious doubt throughout church history. The letter claims his authorship, and objections to it fail to provide convincing arguments.

2. Luther, *Romans*, 71.

3. Cf. Gen 15:6; Rom 4:3, 5, 23–24; Gal 3:6.

Deficiencies in the Justification of the Ungodly

In brief, the traditional Protestant Reformed view of imputed righteousness holds that justification[4] comes by means of a forensic declaration of righteousness from God to the ungodly.[5] This declaration from God imputes the righteousness of Christ through the instrument of faith to the ungodly.[6] The words "reckoned," "imputed," and "credited" are accounting/bookkeeping terms referring to crediting or rendering to someone's account.[7] Righteousness refers to right standing before God and not to ethical

---

4. Grudem, *Systematic Theology*, 723. Justification is a legal declarative act by God whereby the sins of the ungodly stand forgiven based on the the imputed rightousness of Christ. A justified person stands righteous before God.

5. Throughout this book the use of the phrases "traditional Protestant Reformed view," "traditional Protestant view," "Reformed view," and "traditional view," and "Reformed view" indicate the traditional Protestant Reformed doctrinal view of theology, particularly as it pertains to the doctrine of justification, which includes the doctrine of imputed righteousness. The basis of this view of justification developed throughout church history both prior to, but especially after, the Reformation period. The theologians whose writings helped shape the doctrine includes, but is not limited to, Saint Augustine, who wrote about the need for God's grace for salvation, and the justification of sinners. See Augustine, "De Natura et Gratia," 235–36; "Spirit and the Letter," 9, 15, 32, 56. The doctrine of justification, including the doctrine of imputed righteousness, gathers its doctrinal structure from the Protestant Reformation on the writings of Martin Luther, Huldrych Zwingli, Heinrich Bullinger, Martin Bucer, John Calvin and others. The traditional Reformed view of these doctrines continued to develop its orthodoxy after the Reformation, finding crystallization in church creeds and confessions. These confessions and statements include, but are not limited to, the Westminster Confession of Faith and Catechisms and the Heidelberg Catechism. See Westminster Confession, 50–55, 207–11; Heidelberg Catechism, 24–32; cf. Meeks, *Christian Theology*, 2–3; McGrath, *Iustitia Dei*, 39–44; Wright, "Paul of History," 63; Wright, *Justification*, 22–24.

6. Murray, *Redemption*, 121–24; Grudem, *Systematic Theology*, 726–28.

7. Morris, *Romans*, 196–97; Murray, *Redemption*, 131.

virtue. Therefore, God's justification comes through the imputation of the righteousness of Christ by declarative act. The means by which the ungodly receive this gift is through faith.[8]

The imputed righteousness of Christ, by declarative act, is alien to the ungodly because its origin is external; it does not originate from within the ungodly. This alien external righteousness from God brings the ungodly into union with Christ. Therefore, the ungodly stand justified before God based on the redemptive work of Jesus Christ imputed by faith.[9]

In the last few decades, the traditional Reformed view of imputed righteousness has come under heavy scrutiny and disagreement, resulting in an injection of theological fervor centering on the writings of the Apostle Paul. The primary source of this disagreement comes from a theological movement called the New Perspective on Paul (NPP).[10] The NPP movement has come to the forefront of New Testament theological scholarship, resulting in a continuing debate centered on the exegetical interpretation of Paul's writings. To state this more clearly, the debate involves the reinterpretation of Paul's corpus of work found in Holy Scripture based on a new or different perspective.

The NPP encompasses a multifaceted theological rubric that questions the traditional interpretation of the Pauline writings of Scripture, including the doctrine of imputed righteousness.[11] In brief, the NPP seeks to interpret

---

8. Morris, *Romans*, 197, 213–14; Westminster Confession, 51–51, 208–9.

9. Seifrid, "Righteousness Language," 70–71; Lovelace, *Spiritual Life*, 98.

10. Unless otherwise stated, the abbreviation NPP and the phrase "new perspective" will refer to the New Perspective on Paul.

11. Carson, "Summaries and Conclusions," 505.

Deficiencies in the Justification of the Ungodly

the Pauline writings from a first-century Jewish point of view. The new perspective is extremely critical of the traditional view of the Pauline writings, accusing it of having a sixteenth-century bias, which in turn distorts Paul's original meaning.[12]

Currently, one of the foremost advocates for the NPP is N. T. Wright.[13] Wright, an evangelical Christian New Testament scholar, strongly criticizes the traditional interpretation of the Pauline writings, including the doctrine of imputed righteousness. It is Wright's contention that the traditional view of imputed righteousness is in error because of its sixteenth-century interpretation of these writings, which distorts Paul's original meaning.[14]

While Wright agrees with tradition that imputed righteousness is a forensic declarative act by God, the doctrinal similarities end at that point. In brief, Wright does not believe that God's declaration imputes the righteousness of Christ to the ungodly. Rather, God's declarative pronouncement places the fallen sinner in right covenant standing based on God's covenant faithfulness. For Wright, the sinner (those in God's covenant family) makes an appeal to God (the Judge), who renders a decree of righteousness in favor of his covenant people, thereby placing them in right covenant standing.[15] Wright equates this forensic decree to Daniel 9, particularly verse 7, and the covenant language found in Deuteronomy 27–29. Because of Israel's

---

12. Ibid.; Wright, *Justification*, 36–37; Wright, *What Saint Paul Really Said*, 113–14; Wright, "Paul of History," 78–80, 84.

13. Bailey, "Wright Retiring." On August 31, 2010, Wright retired as bishop of Durham. His primary focus is on full-time academic studies. He is the chair of New Testament studies at St. Andrews University, Scotland.

14. Wright, "Paul of History," 78.

15. Wright, *What Saint Paul Really Said*, 96–99.

Introduction

sinfulness, God is righteous in cursing her for violating her covenant with him and sending her into the Babylonian exile. Upon Israel's covenant appeal, God is righteous in blessing Israel by restoring her back to right covenant standing and thereby releasing her from her Babylonian exile.[16]

Further, according to Wright, justification is about *ecclesiology* rather than *soteriology*. Wright rejects the notion that God (Christ) the Judge somehow transfers his righteousness to the ungodly, calling it a category mistake.[17] Justification for Wright is not about getting into the covenant family (i.e., salvation for the sinner). Rather, justification is about how to tell who is in the covenant family.[18] This is not the traditional Reformed view of imputed righteousness. Wright obfuscates his view by acknowledging that Christ bore the sins of the many, which is the imputation of sins to Christ,[19] while at the same time rejecting the imputation of Christ's righteousness to sinners for the justification of the ungodly.

The debate between the traditional Reformed view and Wright's view of the doctrine of imputed righteousness reveals major differences in theology. Succinctly stated, Wright does not believe that Christ imputes (credits) his righteousness to sinners for their justification. He does not believe that the declaration of righteousness reckons anything to the sinner for salvation through the justifying work of Christ.[20] Rather, he believes that the declaration is only a pronouncement that the sinner is now in "right" covenant standing within God's family. Wright's view of this doctrine

16. Wright, *Justification*, 62–63.
17. Wright, *What Saint Paul Really Said*, 96–99, 119; cf. Wright, *Mark*, 233.
18. Ibid., 119.
19. Wright, *Justification*, 136.
20. Wright, *What Saint Paul Really Said*, 96–99, 117.

appears subtle; however, there are major differences in theology that are counter to the traditional Reformed view of Scripture. Wright does not believe that justification through the declaration of righteousness imputed to the ungodly sinner is salvific in terms of receiving credit from Christ's obedience unto death (soteriology).[21] Rather, he believes that the declaration of righteousness places the covenant member back in right covenant standing and is thereby salvific (ecclesiology).[22] However, he makes no allowances for any exchange between the sinner and the righteous obedience of Christ. In fact, it is Wright's view that nothing in the gospel message (in the Pauline writings) has to do with how people receive salvation or how someone becomes a Christian. Rather, Wright claims that the gospel message in the Pauline writings primarily addresses "the proclamation of the Lordship of Jesus Christ."[23]

This book will examine, from a traditional Reformed view, these differences focusing on three areas. First, it will examine Wright's view on its forensic premise. Second, it will examine the lack of exchange or imputation between Christ and the ungodly, per Wright's claim. Third, it will examine Wright's emphasis on ecclesiology rather that soteriology.

The task of trying to understand the implication of imputed righteousness to all who believe is a daunting challenge. The study of biblical and historical theology demonstrates the church's struggle to define Paul's meaning regarding this doctrine. The purpose of this book is to evaluate Wright's view of this doctrine. The importance of this evaluation is to gain hermeneutical clarification for the

21. Wright, *Justification*, 134–35.

22. Wright, *What Saint Paul Really Said*, 119; Wright, *Justification*, 242.

23. Wright, *Justification*, 60, 90, 133, 153.

study of imputed righteousness. The basis of establishing a clearer understanding of the Pauline writings regarding imputed righteousness enlightens, through the power of the Holy Spirit, the Christian understanding of the justifying work of God through Jesus Christ.

The first step in understanding Wright's view of imputed righteousness is to investigate some background information on the NPP movement. Gaining a fundamental understanding of the NPP movement will lay the foundation for understanding Wright's view of imputed righteousness, as explained by Pauline scholars such as Krister Stendahl, E. P. Sanders, and James Dunn. The writings of these scholars have a definite influence on Wright's new perspective view. Wright's view of imputed righteousness coincides with his stance on the NPP movement. This book will not address every nuance of the NPP, but merely provide foundational information of Wright's mindset, the basis of which forms his viewpoint on the doctrine of imputed righteousness.

The next step is to define Wright's view of imputed righteousness. To accomplish this step requires an examination of his writings on this subject per his new perspective influences. Further, defining Wright's view encompasses a summary of his NPP view, which frames his grievance against the traditional view of imputed righteousness. This step provides the framework that establishes his view of this doctrine, which is broken down into three main parts: covenant, law court, and eschatology.

After defining Wright's view of imputed righteousness, the next step is to gain a clear understanding of the traditional Reformed view as it currently stands. This step begins by examining how the early church fathers struggled and dealt with this doctrine, and then looking at how this doctrine developed to become the traditional view. Gaining a clear understanding of the traditional view of imputed

Deficiencies in the Justification of the Ungodly

righteousness will help address the many dogmatic caricatures lodged against the traditional view by Wright.

The final step in evaluating Wright's view of imputed righteousness is to examine the three areas of disagreement from a traditional Reformed viewpoint. First, examine Wright's view on its forensic premise. Second, examine the lack of exchange or imputation between Christ and the ungodly, per Wright's claim. Third, examine Wright's emphasis on ecclesiology rather that soteriology.

1

An Excursus into the New Perspective on Paul

THE FIRST STEP IN understanding N. T. Wright's view of imputed righteousness begins by obtaining a fundamental understanding of the NPP movement. This begins by getting an overview of the movement with a focus on its main characteristics. This will also involve a study of biblical, historical, and theological scholars such as Krister Stendahl, E. P. Sanders, and James D. G. Dunn, who were instrumental in laying the groundwork for the movement and influencing Wright's new perspective view. Wright's new perspective philosophy certainly shapes his understanding of imputed righteousness.

The NPP movement is at times complex in its exegetical analysis and vastly diverse in its theological scope. It covers a wide range of theological themes found throughout the Apostle Paul's corpus of work in Holy Scripture. The NPP has become a multifaceted movement of theological viewpoints. At times, these theological viewpoints do not agree.[1] New Testament theologian Dunn, whom many scholars credit as coining the phrase the "New Perspective on Paul," explains that the NPP is not a dogma that is binding, nor is it symbolic of some school of thought.[2] Rather, the intent of the NPP is to complement other views of the Pauline writings in order to obtain a much fuller and richer understanding of the gospel message.[3]

Many NPP scholars, such as Stendahl, Sanders, and Dunn, focus their attention on Paul's more polarizing themes. These themes include "the relationship between the new covenant and old, the relationship between being 'in Christ' and being a Jew (or even a Pharisee), the relationship between the grace of God in Christ and being under the law."[4] The central theme surrounding the NPP movement has to do with Judaism and not Paul per se.[5] The primary intent of NPP scholars is to change the mindset of how contemporary theologians view the Pauline writings as it pertains to Judaism during the first century.

KRISTER STENDAHL

The Peril of Modernization

The NPP traces its roots to a Harvard professor named Krister Stendahl,[6] who on September 3, 1961, delivered an

1. Carson, "Summaries and Conclusions," 505.
2. Dunn, *New Perspective on Paul*, 100.
3. Ibid., ix–xi.
4. Carson, "Mystery and Fulfillment," 393.
5. Westerholm, "New Perspective at Twenty-Five," 2.

6. See Stendahl, "Krister Stendahl 1921–2008." Stendahl passed away on April 15, 2008. At the time of his death, Stendahl was the Andrew W. Mellon Professor of Divinity Emeritus at Harvard Divinity School.

An Excursus into the New Perspective on Paul

address entitled "The Apostle Paul and the Introspective Conscience of the West"[7] to the American Psychological Association at their annual meeting. In this presentation, Stendahl attempts to address the dangers of interpreting history and historical documents such as biblical text with the presumption that "man [humanity] remains basically the same through the ages."[8] It is in this vein that Stendahl criticizes Western theologians for committing eisegesis by reading a contemporary Western cultural introspective consciousness into the Pauline epistles. This section will provide a general summary of Stendahl's address and the influence it has on the new perspective movement.

The primary focus of the address deals with Romans 7:14–25. The thrust of the argument focuses on Paul's statement, "For I do not do the good I want, but the evil I do not want is what I do." For years, Western theologians have read into this passage an introspective guilty conscience inferring that Paul struggled with a guilty conscience. It is for this reason that Western theologians hail the apostle "as a hero of the introspective conscience."[9] The Western introspective conscience is comparable to what psychologist Carl Gustav Jung[10] calls "individuation," in that these

---

7. Stendahl, *Paul among Jews*, 78. The address presented to the American Psychological Association was a revised edition of an article by Stendahl entitled "Paulus och Samvetet," published in the Swedish journal *Svensk Exegetisk Årsbok* 25 (1960) 62–77.

8. Stendahl, *Paul among Jews*, 79.

9. Ibid.

10. "Carl Gustav Jung," *Columbia Encyclopedia*, 2008. Jung (1875–1961), a Swiss psychiatrist, was a contempory to Sigmund Freud. His primary studies dealt most with the unconscious. He summarized that the unconscious state of a person is divided into the personal and archetypal dimensions. A person becomes complete when he/she obtains a conscious and unconscious harmony called individuation.

Deficiencies in the Justification of the Ungodly

views seek an internal answer, in a person's consciousness or unconsciousness, to an individual or societal struggle.[11]

David Cox's work entitled *Jung and St. Paul: A Study of the Doctrine of Justification by Faith and Its Relation to the Concept of Individuation* helps identify and provides solutions to the Western problem of a guilty conscience. In this book Cox makes a comparative study of how psychology and religion relate in the human psychic. According to Cox, both the Apostle Paul and Jung agree that each human struggles with and relies on his/her own inner conscious devices when confronting a dilemma. Cox goes as far as stating that the word *sin* in a religious setting and the *manifestation of the unconscious* in the psychotherapeutic setting bear the same meaning with regard to the effect on the human psyche.[12]

The introspective interpretation of the Pauline epistles is purely Western in nature and not the Apostle Paul's original intended meaning for his biblical writings. The modernization of Pauline scripture is a produce of Western Christianity in its quest to satisfy the guilty conscience.[13] Henry Cadbury gives an excellent summary of the implications of modernizing biblical text in his book entitled *The Peril of Modernizing Jesus*. Modernization of the biblical text presupposes the notion that humans and their environments remain unchanged throughout history. The perils of this presupposition can affect the modern exegete's understanding and biases of the biblical text.[14] One of the

---

11. Jung, *Two Essays*, 100. Jung defines individuation as a destination where a human becomes an individual by embracing their "innermost, last, and incomparable uniqueness." It is a "coming to selfhood or self-realization."

12. Cox, *Jung and St. Paul*, preface, 18, 28.

13. Stendahl, *Paul among Jews*, 78–79.

14. Cadbury, *Peril of Modernizing Jesus*, v–vi.

An Excursus into the New Perspective on Paul

possible causes examined by Cadbury for the modernization problem incurred by many theologians has to do with the natural unconscious tendency to make biblical text real. In other words, modernization gives the reader a better understanding of the text. Cadbury equates this to a modern painting depicting a biblical event.[15] This tendency results in erroneous assumptions regarding the true meaning of the text.

The point to all this is that Western Christianity (particularly Protestantism), in its quest to modernize biblical text, misinterprets the Pauline epistles, particularly the statements regarding *justification by faith*, resulting in the loss of their original meaning. Martin Luther bears the blame for initiating this misinterpretation, which for centuries sidetracked Western theologians on an exegetical path that the Apostle Paul never intended.[16]

Luther, in an effort to make the Pauline writings more meaningful to his contemporaries, modernized these writings so that they would better relate to his personal struggles with guilt (i.e., his introspective conscience). Luther's introspective conscience captured the imagination of sixteenth-century Western theologians, who viewed Paul's statements regarding justification by faith as the common denominator between the experiences of humanity and Paul. Hence, the presupposition that humanity remains the same throughout history renders the text its modernized meaning. Luther's misinterpretation of the Pauline epistles is a classic example of someone reading his sixteenth-century presuppositions into first-century writings. Luther answered a question that was vital to his contemporaries who were seeking to find a gracious God. Luther found the answer to this question in the Pauline writings of justification

15. Ibid., 28.
16. Stendahl, *Paul among Jews*, 79–96.

Deficiencies in the Justification of the Ungodly

by faith in Jesus Christ. However, while Luther's response to his contemporaries demonstrates a good example of how biblical theology can and does develop throughout the centuries, it is not the primary theme of Paul's original writings regarding justification. From its inception and continuing through modernity, Luther's misinterpretation of justification by faith established a new biblical ideology that has led Western theologians astray.[17]

Contrary to Luther and Protestantism's belief, the primary theme of the Pauline writings regarding justification is the inclusion of Gentiles with Jews into God's covenant family. Israel's unfaithfulness as a nation to the covenant proves beneficial to the Gentiles. Luther's introspective guilt of his disobedience to the law found its escape from the wrath of God in his interpretation of the Pauline writings on justification by faith. However, this view of justification is a sixteenth-century view and does not fully grasp the magnitude of the Pauline letters.[18]

Luther's view of justification by faith also does not take into consideration the issues facing nascent Christians (both Jews and Gentiles). Nascent Jewish Christians[19] of Paul's day were aware of the impossibility to perfectly maintaining the law, but knew that the law has a built-in

17. Ibid., 79.

18. Ibid., 80.

19. Early followers of Christ did not use the designation "Christian." Antiochenes of Syria first used the word as a designation of the people who followed Christ. See Acts 11:26; Chance, "Christian," 239–40. Nascent Christians, who were mostly if not all Jews, considered themselves to be a sect of Judaism. They believed that the Messiah had come and ushered in the messianic age. They continued to observe certain Jewish laws such as worshiping in the temple and on the Sabbath day. Problems regarding the Law increased as more and more Gentiles began to populate the church; hence the issue involving the Law written about by the Pauline epistles; cf. Gonzalez, *Story of Christianity*, 19–22.

An Excursus into the New Perspective on Paul

component of God's grace. Because of God's forgiveness, through repentance, failure to maintain the law will not result in condemnation. Paul makes this point perfectly clear by demonstrating a "robust,"[20] not an introspective conscience throughout his writings. In Philippians 3, Paul writes about his reason for having confidence in the flesh and his *blameless* status regarding the righteousness of the law.[21] Even his persecution of the church, prior to the Damascus road encounter with Jesus, does not lessen Paul's zealous confidence in fulfilling God's law as a righteous Jewish Pharisee.[22] Paul's behavior is a clear demonstration of God's built-in grace as it pertains to the law given to the Jews.

The law convicted Luther of sin due to his introspective guilt conscience, which saw no escape from the wrath of God. This introspective conviction by the law set the framework for Luther's theology regarding justification by faith. Luther, and his contemporaries, found great comfort and liberation to their problem of guilt in the Pauline writings of justification by faith. While this is the problem that faced Luther and his contemporaries, this is not the problem that faced first-century Jews, nor is it the intended meaning of the Pauline writings.[23]

Luther's introspective view of the Pauline writings came from his Augustinian monastic roots. Saint Augustine, in his writings, also demonstrates an obvious introspective guilt regarding the law, which reflects a

20. Stendahl, *Paul among Jews*, 80–81.

21. Thielman, "Law," 529. The Apostle Paul uses the word "Law" in his writings to refer to the Torah or the *Nomos* (Jewish customs, e.g., circumcision); Matthews, "Law," 793–95. The Law functioned as personal or communal statutes for Israel.

22. Stendahl, *Paul among Jews*, 80–81.

23. Ibid., 80–83.

hermeneutical misinterpretation of Scripture that accuses first-century Jews of legalism.[24] However, legalism was not a concern for first-century Jews who believed that they were in God's covenant family. The Torah, for first-century Jews, did not bring death but repentance, which brought grace for eternal life. It is clear that first-century Jews would reject Luther's introspective interpretation of the Pauline writings regarding the law. First-century Jews realized that Paul was addressing first-century Gentile followers of Christ and not Jews.[25]

Paul, a Pharisee of Pharisees, with his knowledge of the Torah, would not infer that the law brings death to Israel.[26] Rather, the "death" spoken about has to do with justification by faith for the Gentile followers of Christ, who through Christ are now a part of God's covenant family.[27] Paul, being the apostle to the Gentiles, grapples with the question of the law as it pertains to Gentiles in God's plan and in God's church (covenant family).[28] As a part of God's covenant family, nascent Gentile Christians who did not originally receive the law are now aware of its conviction and its original demands upon the Jews.

In his biblical writings, Paul is dealing with the problem of the law as it pertains to the relationship between Jewish and Gentile Christ-followers.[29] Paul explains that now that the Messiah has arrived, through justification by faith, a new relationship exists between Jews and Gentiles tantamount to a new definition of Israel.[30] Paul's defense of

24. Ibid., 83, 85–87.
25. Gager, *Reinventing Paul*, 43–44.
26. Ibid., 44.
27. Stanton, "Paul's Gospel," 179.
28. Stendahl, *Paul among Jews*, 84.
29. Ibid.
30. Davies, *Jewish and Pauline*, 128–29.

An Excursus into the New Perspective on Paul

his mission to the Gentiles and the doctrine of justification by faith is a "scriptural argument, according to the exegetical principles of Judaism."[31] At the time, Paul is dealing with Jewish law issues and Judaizers who want new converts to adhere to the law, which includes circumcision. Paul is not trying to start a new religion. Rather, he is trying to explain how Gentiles who did not receive the law are now a part of God's covenant people.[32] The basis of his explanation is the arrival of the Messiah and the impact this arrival has on the law.

Theologian H. J. Schoeps' writings on Jewish rabbinical history reflected in Pauline theology addresses the abolition of the law in light of the death and resurrection of Jesus Christ.[33] In accordance to his rabbinical training, the Apostle must make logical inferences regarding the Torah with the arrival of the messianic age in the person of Jesus Christ, who fulfills the law.[34] Paul writes in Romans, "For Christ is the end of the law so that there may be righteousness for everyone who believes" (Rom. 10:4). Hence, the major theme of the Pauline writings regarding justification by faith has to do with the inclusion of Gentiles aside from the law into God's covenant family.

Western contemporary theologians misinterpret Paul's primary theme in this area because they focus their attention on human depravity from an introspective viewpoint and the notion that the law brings death. This is not the problem that faced Paul and his Jewish contemporaries. They believed that "to the one who performs it the Torah is *sam hayyim* (a medicine of life); to the one who does it not,

---

31. Stendahl, "Judaism and Christianity," 6.
32. Ibid.
33. Schoeps, *Paul*, 171–75.
34. Ibid., 171.

Deficiencies in the Justification of the Ungodly

it is a *sam muth* (a poison)."[35] Paul and his contemporaries knew that the law is good. Paul writes that the "Law is holy, and the commandment is holy and just and good" (Rom 7:12).

It is emphatically clear that Romans 7:19,[36] a verse so often quoted by traditional theologians as proof of Paul's introspection, is Paul's testimony to the goodness and holiness of the law. When examining the verse it is clear that the verse is not addressing a pre-Christian or mature Christian experience.[37] It is Paul's defense of the holiness of the law and the utter wickedness of sin.[38]

Western theologians, such as Luther, have taken this passage and made it the focal point of human depravity. The law "became the incidental framework around the golden truth of Pauline anthropology."[39] What is a supporting theme regarding the goodness of the law reaches a theological height in Western Christian doctrine. The theme of justification by faith written about in the Pauline writings is ecclesiological not soteriological. Neither sin nor an introspective guilty conscience is a concern for Paul. Those

---

35. Rabbi Joshua ben Levi, Yoma 72b, quoted in Schoeps, *Paul*, 175.

36. "For I do not do the good I want, but the evil I do not want is what I do."

37. Mitton, "Romans VII Reconsidered—I," 78. Stendahl makes reference to C. Leslie Mitton's article about Rom 7:14–25, particularly 7:19. According to Mitton, many theologians believe that Paul is addressing his pre-conversion, pre-Christian experience. This view is appealing to many Christians, who can relate to it from a biblical and personal perspective (Mitton, "Romans VII Reconsidered—II"). According to Mitton, other theologians believe that Paul is addressing the view of a mature Christian (Mitton, "Romans VII Reconsidered—III"). Mitton offers a third view of this passage that blends the strong points of both the pre-Christian and mature Christian viewpoints.

38. Stendahl, *Paul among Jews*, 91–94.

39. Ibid., 93.

who are members of God's covenant people will remain members and receive salvation. Paul's primary concern in this passage is twofold. First, his weakened physical condition amidst his messianic directive to the Gentiles is a hindrance. Second, he grieves his fellow Jews' rejection of the message proclaiming the arrival of the Messiah.[40] It is not his introspective guilty conscience. The climax to the letter to the Romans comes in chapters 9–11, where Paul answers the Jew/Gentile question regarding the kingdom of God.[41]

Stendahl concludes his lecture to the American Psychological Association by accusing Western theologians of taking a secondary theological issue and giving it a primary theological status. Reading the Pauline writings in its original context opens up "a new perspective for systematic theology and practical theology."[42] He warns against the assumption that humans remain the same throughout history and proclaims liberation for those who can set aside their presuppositions in order to gain a better understanding of the original biblical text.

E. P. SANDERS

Covenantal Nomism

After Stendahl, E. P. Sanders continues the new perspective study of the Pauline writings by researching the rabbinic Judaism of antiquity.[43] His study of Judaism regarding the law and its relationship to the covenant centers on Palestinian

40. Stendahl, *Final Account*, 1.
41. Stendahl, *Paul among Jews*, 85.
42. Ibid., 95–96.
43. "Duke Religion Professor E.P. Sanders." Ed Parish Sanders is currently professor emeritus at Duke University's Department of Religion. He has written extensively in the area of first-century Judaism.

Deficiencies in the Justification of the Ungodly

Judaism during the period of 200 BCE through 200 CE.[44] In 1977, Sanders' book[45] ushered in a new perspective view of the Pauline scriptures, which in turn brought into being a multitude of studies under the same rubric, ultimately called the NPP.[46] The new perspective reading of Paul's writings, according to some theological scholars, including D. A. Carson, is "the reigning paradigm."[47]

The conclusions made in Sanders' book have influenced New Testament studies especially in the area of the Pauline writings. Sanders' studies into rabbinic Judaism lead him to oppose the belief that the Judaism of Paul's day was a "legalistic works-righteousness" religion.[48] Rather, he believes that *works of the law* are a response to God's grace.[49] This section will provide a general summary of Sanders' influence in the new perspective movement.

The Jews of Paul's day believed that they stood justified before God as his covenant nation, Israel.[50] They maintained and demonstrated their justified standing before God by their works. Paul's theology is consistent with Palestinian Judaism in regard to salvation. Both Paul and Palestinian Judaism agree that salvation is by God alone. However, God's righteous *judgment* for Palestinian Judaism comes by staying in God's covenant through works. When it comes to the two aspects of the "relationship between grace and works: *salvation is by grace but judgment is according to*

---

44. Sanders, *Paul and Palestinian Judaism*, xi, 419.

45. Ibid.

46. Carson, "Summaries and Conclusions," 505.

47. Ibid.

48. Duncan, "Attractions of the New Perspective(s) on Paul," Sanders, *Paul and Palestinian Judaism*, 33.

49. Sanders, *Paul and Palestinian Judaism*, 543.

50. Westerholm, "New Perspective at Twenty-Five," 2.

An Excursus into the New Perspective on Paul

works; works are the condition of remaining 'in' but they do not earn salvation."[51]

The writings of W. D. Davies detail the demands of the law on the covenant people. Davies explains that the covenant relationship between God and Israel demands obedience to the law. However, because of God's grace, disobedience does not void it.[52] Israel indeed realizes that its salvation is in the hands of Yahweh not in the obedience of the law. The law is a holy gift from God for those who desire to remain in the covenant.

The sacrificial system provides atonement for the sins of those in the covenant who fail to keep the law. Conversely, there are indeed those Jews whose desire it is to live outside this covenant. Judaism, at the time, did not concern itself with those Jews.[53] Davies' description of God's covenant with Israel is a pattern of *covenantal nomism*.[54] The structure and pattern of covenantal nomism is as follows.

> (1) God has chosen Israel and (2) given the law. The law implies both (3) God's promise to maintain the election and (4) the requirement to obey. (5) God rewards obedience and punishes transgression. (6) The law provides for means of atonement, and atonement results in (7) maintenance or re-establishment of the covenantal relationship. (8) All those who are maintained in the covenant by obedience, atonement and God's mercy belong to the group which will be saved.[55]

---

51. Sanders, *Paul and Palestinian Judaism*, 543.
52. Davies, *Jewish and Pauline Studies*, 17–18.
53. Ibid., 17–20.
54. Sanders, *Paul and Palestinian Judaism*, 511.
55. Ibid., 422.

Deficiencies in the Justification of the Ungodly

Covenantal nomism describes God's interworking relationship with Israel. God initiates the relationship (the Divine covenant), and Israel responds (the human response) with obedience to the covenant.[56] In other words, all Israel's faithful covenant members who obey God's law, which includes repentance and maintenance of the sacrificial law, receive atonement for their transgressions. God's elect do not need to obtain salvation but rather only need to demonstrate their membership in God's covenant family through obedience to the law.[57] This is not salvation via merits but rather the badge of membership in God's covenant family.

H. A. A. Kennedy calls the law "the crowning proof of Israel's election . . . its acknowledgement of the Divine grace."[58] Israel knows that the law is divine in its origin and therefore good. Further, they do not view the law as an imposition or burden but seek to maintain it with joy.[59] However, sin, whether intentional or not, is disobedience to God's law.[60]

Because of sin, Israel is aware of their need for divine grace to maintain their membership in God's covenant family. They know that the law does not empower them with the ability to observe the law.[61] For the most part, disobedience to the covenant comes when the rigors of maintaining the law lead to the pursuit of personal merit, which eventually surpasses the grace of God that sustains it.[62] This is all a result of sin in the world, which is a power that is

56. Dunn, *New Perspective*, 6.

57. Ibid., 236.

58. Kennedy, "Significance and Range," 392, Sanders, *Paul and Palestinian Judaism*, 419–20.

59. Sanders, *Paul and Palestinian Judaism*, 110.

60. Ibid., 111–12.

61. Sanders, *Paul, the Law*, 73–75.

62. Sanders, *Paul and Palestinian Judaism*, 420.

An Excursus into the New Perspective on Paul

alien to God. Sin uses the law as its agent for disobedience.[63] It is for this reason that the purpose of the law is twofold. First, the law is not for Israel's salvation but merely serves as a "pedagogue until Christ."[64] Second, God gives the law to condemn the entire world (save Israel) so that salvation can come through faith in Christ.[65]

Paul understands the role of the law in Judaism. However, because of the advent of the Messiah, Paul seeks to explain the abolishment of the law as it pertains to salvation and the inclusion of Gentiles into God's covenant family. For Paul, Christ came to save both the Jews and the Gentiles. It is now faith in Christ that leads to salvation for the Gentiles, rather than coming under the law. For Jews, being a covenant member rather than in Christ is an oversimplification of the role of the Messiah in the salvation of the Gentiles. The human plight involves transgressions against God. The solution to the plight comes with the death of Christ, which cleanses these transgressions.

The coming of the Messiah modifies the original concept of covenantal nomism in two main areas. First, Paul declares Jesus Christ as Lord over all. Everyone who believes in him will receive salvation. Second, Christ declares Paul the apostle to the Gentiles. Further, the terms *faith* and *righteousness* in the Pauline writings take on more than one definition. To begin with, Paul applies more than one meaning to the word *faith*. He does so to rebuff the claims of the law. The theological use of the term *faith* for Christians is counter to Judaism's use of the word. Faith is a response to Christ's salvation, *apart from the law*. It

---

63. Sanders, *Paul, the Law*, 73–75.
64. Ibid., 66.
65. Sanders, *Paul and Palestinian Judaism*, 497.

Deficiencies in the Justification of the Ungodly

excludes *boasting* but is not opposite to it. Faith is *trust* but is not exactly trusting.[66]

Paul's use of the word *righteousness* also takes on several different meanings depending on the context. The righteousness of God demonstrates his right action and power. It can also refer to his faithfulness, obligation, and his state of being right. Therefore, God's righteousness by faith is not a doctrine with one meaning. Rather, it serves as Paul's argument against obtaining salvation through obedience of the law. The true meaning of *righteousness* in the Pauline epistles, regardless of its grammatical use (viz., verb, adjective or noun) means *life* (Rom 6:16; Gal 3:21) and salvation. It is not a forensic, eschatological, or ethical term.[67]

Righteousness is a term used for those people who are already in God's covenant family. It is not an entry point for believers but rather a term used for maintaining obedience to the law. Righteousness (justification) by faith and being in or participating in Christ amount to the same thing. Therefore, righteousness by faith is not a doctrine in and of itself. As such, there is no need for an imputed righteousness in a traditional sense, because a person stands righteous if he/she is already in God's covenant family. Imputed righteousness is *fictional* in that it is a misinterpretation of Paul's view of righteousness by Luther and other Western theologians. They read an introspective and individual view into the term, which is not Paul's intent.[68]

There is a need to set the record straight. The traditional view of Judaism as being a works-righteousness religion is a misinterpretation of Scripture. God chose Israel as his covenant people. As members of God's covenant family, there is no need to gain God's favor through works

66. Ibid.
67. Ibid.
68. Ibid; Sanders, *Paul*, 78–96.

righteousness. Works of the law demonstrate Israel's membership in this covenant.[69]

Thomas R. Schreiner, a NT professor, writes the following regarding Sanders' assessment of Israel's obedience to the work: "First God redeems Israel from Egypt, and then he gives the law, so obedience to the law is a response to God's grace, not an attempt to gain righteousness by works (see Ex. 19–20)."[70] This is perhaps Sanders' most important work in the NPP. He seeks to change the traditional view of Judaism in the Pauline writings and correct the negative caricatures made against it.

JAMES D. G. DUNN

The New Perspective on Paul

James D. G. Dunn[71] follows Sanders in viewing the Pauline writings from a new perspective. Many theologians credit him with coining the now-widely-known phrase *New Perspective on Paul*. However, Wright points out that both he and Dunn borrowed the phrase from Stendahl.[72] This section will provide a general summary of Dunn's influence in the new perspective movement.

Dunn shares many philosophical areas of agreement with Stendahl and Sanders regarding the new perspective movement; however, two main areas of disagreement come

---

69. Sanders, *Paul and Palestinian Judaism*, 420.

70. Schreiner, *Apostle of God's Glory*, 117–18.

71. "Staff Profile: Professor James D. G. Dunn." Dunn is currently professor emeritus at Durham University's Department of Theology and Religion. He has written academic jounal articles. His research interest include Christian origin, Jewish/Christian relations, New Testament exegesis and Theology, and the use of the Bible.

72. Wright, *Justification*, 28.

Deficiencies in the Justification of the Ungodly

to the forefront. First, contrary to the belief of Stendahl and Sanders, Paul's writings about the law are not contradictory or inconsistent. Paul's view of the law, however complicated, is harmonious and consistent throughout his writings.[73] Theological scholars such as Guy Prentiss Waters and J. Ligon Duncan believe that Dunn takes his new perspective view and formulates an in-depth exegetical analysis of the Pauline writings.[74]

Second, according to Dunn, there is a failure by Sanders "to grasp the full significance of *the social function of the law*."[75] The full social function of the law has an influence on Paul and the issues that he faces. These social functions are characteristics that provide a social group such as Israel with its own identifying features. Some groups also associate these characteristics as identifying boundaries. For Judaism, these identifying characteristics come in the form of *works of the law*, which demonstrate covenant membership. The traditional view of covenantal nomism misinterprets these works as works righteousness performed in order to obtain salvation rather than as a demonstration of it.[76]

In its basic form, *works of the law* simply means the *deeds* (actions) required of God's chosen people by the law. The law is the Jewish law, the Mosaic Torah. Israel's part in its covenant with God comes in the form of works of the law. It is their obedience to the grace given to them by Yahweh. The law gives Israel a *sense of privilege* in that it is God's way of setting Israel apart from the Gentiles. The role of the law in the Pauline writings is that of a governess or tutor that provides protective guidance for Israel. The law

---

73. Dunn, *New Perspective*, 121–22.

74. Waters, *Justification and the New Perspective*, 96; Duncan, "Attractions of the New Perspective(s)."

75. Dunn, *New Perspective*, 122.

76. Ibid., 122–23.

An Excursus into the New Perspective on Paul

is a power of its own that Israel is under. In a sense, the law is a guardian over God's people. Therefore, *works of the law* carries a meaning of obedience for covenant's sake not for salvation's sake.[77]

In regards to the means of effecting justification, Paul stresses *faith* not works of the law. Faith is the means by which individuals and people groups experience the gospel. The dispute over works of the law occurs with the involvement of Gentiles. Justification by faith is the means by which Gentiles receive acceptance into God's covenant family. More than that, it demonstrates humans' utter dependency on God. This dependency on God and God alone defines Paul's statement of justification by faith alone. This dependency by God's elect through works reveals faith and trust in God who justifies. Adam failed to demonstrate this trust and dependency in God but Abraham did not fail. Abraham trusted God and gave him glory. It is this faith that God reckons as righteousness. Justification, therefore, is God's initial acceptance of the sinner into covenantal relationship. However, it does not end with this initial step but continues throughout the life of the sinner, who demonstrates his/her covenant membership with obedience (works). Obedience is a necessary part of justification, which culminates in the final acquittal.[78]

The death of Jesus Christ plays a representative role and not a substitutionary role in its relationship to justification. Christ's death on the cross was not one of atonement where Christ died to free sinners. Rather, Christ's death on the cross represented the death of the sins of the flesh. Believing sinners do not escape death but rather share in Christ's death on the cross. Paul, however, does use *cultic* sacrificial language taken from Leviticus 4 and 16, but the

77. Dunn, *Theology of Paul*, 137–43, 355.
78. Ibid., 371–72, 379, 386–89.

Deficiencies in the Justification of the Ungodly

language Paul uses is one of "the neutralization of a life-threatening virus than of anger appeased by punishment."[79]

Paul also uses metaphoric terms in his writings, such as *sacrifice*, *representation*, *redemption*, and *reconciliation*, to express the death of Christ.[80] These terms are not literal and Christ's death on the cross is not a literal sacrifice by and to God. It is a mistake to raise any single metaphors used in the Pauline writings to primary or even normative status and expect all other metaphors in Paul's writing to meet the same distinctive characteristics.[81]

The NPP movement receives much of its identifying features from Stendahl, Sanders, and Dunn. These summaries of their NPP views provide a basis for understanding Wright's view of the NPP movement, which encapsulates his view of imputed righteousness. Chapter 2 will provide a summary of Wright's view of the NPP and will detail his view of imputed righteousness.

---

79. Ibid., 214–15, 385–86.
80. Dunn, *New Perspective*, 97, 258.
81. Dunn, *Theology of Paul*, 332.

2

N. T. Wright

THE NEW PERSPECTIVE ON PAUL

THE NEXT STEP IN evaluating N. T. Wright's view of imputed righteousness comes by obtaining a comprehensive understanding of his view on this doctrine. To accomplish this task requires an examination of his writings on this subject per his new perspective influences. This begins by gaining a general understanding of his view of the NPP movement. This then continues by examining his new perspective view of the Pauline writings on the doctrine of imputed righteousness.

Wright, in the last few years, has become one of the foremost advocates of the NPP movement.[1] Although he readily admits that there is no such thing as a new viewpoint or perspective regarding the Pauline writings, he

---

1. Bailey, "N. T. Wright Retiring."

Deficiencies in the Justification of the Ungodly

does admit that there is a "family of perspectives,"[2] with many different viewpoints (some fundamentally different) regarding these writings. At times, he tries to distance himself from other NPP scholars such as Sanders and Dunn on certain theological issues. Nevertheless, he refers to these disagreements as family squabbles, "sibling rivalries going on inside."[3] According to Wright, his collected works on the Pauline letters are not attempts "to defend something monolithic called the new perspective,"[4] but rather to bring about scholarly debate in this area of biblical study. Wright, an evangelical Christian, strongly criticizes the traditional view of the Pauline writings regarding justification, including the traditional view of imputed righteousness. This chapter provides a general summary of Wright's NPP view on the doctrine of justification, which includes the doctrine of imputed righteousness.

In general, according to Wright, the traditional view of justification is in error because of its sixteenth-century interpretative origin, which erroneously distorts Paul's message by misrepresenting Paul's first-century audience. Clearly stated, "[T]he tradition of Pauline interpretation has manufactured a false Paul by manufacturing a false Judaism for him to oppose."[5] Tradition does not place Paul's writings on the subject of justification in its proper first-century Jewish context. The Pauline letters address issues and concerns of first-century Judaism, which sixteenth-century Protestant theologians distorted. A sixteenth-century perspective on the Pauline letters causes many problems, such as the

---

2. Wright, *Justification*, 28.
3. Ibid., 28–29; Wright, "New Perspective."
4. Wright, *Justification*, 29.
5. Wright, "Paul of History," 78.

tendency to focus on the individual and not on the national perspective.[6]

Both E. P. Sanders and James Dunn affirm the view that first-century Judaism was not what traditional Protestants call a *works–righteousness* religion. Tradition holds the misinterpretation that works righteousness was the means by which first-century Jews performed works of the law to gain salvation. Scripture counters this belief: Israel maintains obedience of the Torah in order to demonstrate and ensure their covenant relationship with God.[7] As affirmed by other new perspective theologians (viz., Sanders and Dunn), *works righteousness* is not a legalistic way of obtaining salvation. On the contrary, it is how first-century Israel demonstrated its assurance of their covenantal relationship with God. It is not an "entrance into"[8] God's covenant family. In concurrence with Sanders, works righteousness is not "so much about soteriology as about ecclesiology."[9] Most new perspective scholars (viz., Stendahl, Sanders, and Dunn) agree that the traditional Protestant confusion in reading Pauline theology, especially in regards to justification, has to do with the Catholic–Protestant debate during the Reformation period.[10]

---

6. Wright, *Justification*, 36–37; Wright, *What Saint Paul Really Said*, 113–14.

7. Wright, *Justification*, 73–74; Wright, "Paul of History," 78.

8. Venema, "What Did Saint Paul Really Say?," 40.

9. Wright, *What Saint Paul Really Said*, 119; Sanders, *Paul and Palestinian*, 424, 544.

10. Scholars such as Stendahl and Sanders believe that the traditional view of justification came about when Protestant theologians during sixteenth century "retrojected" (the term used by Sanders) their Protestant-Catholic debate into the Pauline writings. For traditional theologians, first-century Judaism took on the role of Catholicism and Protestant Chrisitans took on the role of Paul's writings against works of the Law. Note that during the Protestant-Catholic

Deficiencies in the Justification of the Ungodly

The works of the law, as Dunn attests, are Jewish *boundary markers* that clearly distinguish God's covenant people from the Gentiles. These boundary markers demonstrate Israel's *ethnic identity*, a nationalistic identity as God's people.[11] Dunn's new perspective view of works righteousness makes a major breakthrough[12] in helping to gain a better understanding of Ephesians 2 as it relates to works of the law and the division between Jews and Gentiles.[13] Gentiles are heirs along with the Jews of the inheritance. Christ destroyed the wall of separation between Jews and Gentiles, who are now "members of the same body, and partakers of the promise in Christ Jesus through the gospel" (Eph 3:6).[14] The problems with the Judaizers in Galatia had to do with their insistence on maintaining their Jewish national identity through works of the law. Works righteousness for salvation is not the issue in question.[15] It is not what Paul is talking about when he refers to the problem of *boasting*. The problem is the issue of boasting about their national identity, their possession of the Torah, and their superior status in God's plan.[16] Paul's use of the word *boasting* in both Galatians and Romans has to do with faith as the equalizer, which demonstrates membership in God's covenant family. The coming of the Messiah eliminates boasting and there-

---

debate, Catholicism believed that justification began with the work of Christ and continued through a merit system of obedience to the law. Wright, "Paul of History," 80; cf., Ott, *Fundamentals*, 262; Grudem, *Systematic Theology*, 728.

11. Wright, *Justification*, 118, 171–75; Dunn, *New Perspective*, 213–14, 282–84, 422–25.

12. Wright, *Justification*, 172.

13. Ibid.; Dunn, *New Perspective*, 213–26.

14. Wright, *Justification*, 172; Dunn, *New Perspective*, 33.

15. Wright, *Justification*, 243.

16. Ibid., 210–11.

fore eliminates any separation between Jews and Gentiles.[17] The new perspective view of the Pauline writings regarding justification is counter to the traditional view in many areas, including imputed righteousness.

Justification

In order to gain a proper first-century understanding of imputed righteousness, an examination of j*ustification*, including *justification by faith*, is necessary. Gaining a proper understanding begins with a categorical rejection of Luther's statement claiming that the doctrine of justification is the article by which the church stands or falls.[18] Alister McGrath's assessment holds true that salvation comes to humanity by God through Jesus Christ, and any attempt to limit it to one doctrine loses the fullness of Christ's work found in Scripture.[19]

The examination of this doctrine continues with an analysis of the Greek root word for justification, *dikaios*.[20] In Koine Greek,[21] this word can mean right, just, or righteous. The word *dikaiosune* can mean righteousness or justice.[22] It is indeed difficult to translate the root word into the English language, which results in the misinterpretation of Scripture due to the misuse or mistranslation of this word in its

17. Wright, *Climax*, 170–71.
18. Wright, *Justification*, 79.
19. Ibid., 79–80; McGrath, *Iustitia Dei*, 1–2.
20. Mounce, *Biblical Greek*, 308, 430.
21. Ibid., 1. Koine Greek is a simplified version of the classical Greek used during antiquity. It is the Greek used by everyday people during that time.
22. Wright, *What Saint Paul Really Said*, 95; Bromily, *Theological Dictionary*, 169. According to this dictionary, the Greek word for just or justice can also mean correct, good, legal, right, or correct.

Deficiencies in the Justification of the Ungodly

proper context.[23] The misuse of the word *righteousness* adds to the misinterpretation of the traditional view of imputed righteousness. Further, the Greek phrase *dikaiosyne theou* carries the same meaning as the original Hebrew phrase *tsedaqah elohim*,[24] both of which mean God's covenant faithfulness, justice, or "righteousness."[25] No English phrase carries an equivalent meaning for *dikaiosyne theou*.[26] Further, justification in the *here and now* and justification in the *eschaton* are two distinct realms. Faith is the component for both. The demonstration of faith serves as the boundary marker for identifying God's people in the *here and now*. Faith also serves as their belief in God's covenant promises for future justification.[27]

Faith in NT times served as a good-works boundary marker or badge that demonstrated and identified membership into God's covenant family. Good works are not ceremonial rites performed for entrance into God's family.[28] Works are what God's people do to demonstrate their membership in the covenant family. Faith is not a performance that helps a person gain entry into God's covenant family.[29] NT faith echoes the faith found in OT Judaism in the obedience to Torah. Succinctly stated,

> When people believe the gospel of Jesus and his resurrection, and confess him as Lord, they are in fact doing what Torah wanted all along, and

---

23. Wright, *What Saint Paul Really Said*, 95–96.

24. For consistency, all Hebrew words are in their transliterated English spelling unless otherwise stated.

25. Wright, *Paul*, 25.

26. Ibid.

27. Wright, *Justification*, 143–48, 170–72.

28. Wright, *What Saint Paul Really Said*, 124.

29. Wright, *Paul*, 112.

N. T. Wright

are therefore displaying the necessary marks of covenant renewal.[30]

Justification is the declaration of who belongs to God's covenant family; it is not the process of how someone receives salvation.[31] Further, it is through the faithfulness of Christ, *pistis Christou*, that God's plan to rescue the world comes to fruition.[32] *Pistis Christou* is not the faith of humans in Christ, but rather the faithfulness of Christ to fulfill the divine plan of redemption.[33]

Justification by Faith

Traditional Christians today have a mistaken view of the Pauline teachings of justification by faith. They mistakenly view justification by faith from a sixteenth-century proto-Pelagian perspective. This is to say: justification by faith, for contemporary Christians, means that people cannot through their works save themselves. Their works will never be good enough to gain entry into heaven because it is only from the grace of God that salvation comes to the ungodly through faith. Their good works account for nothing. This view of justification by faith is somewhat *misleading* and *distorted*. It certainly does not convey the full meaning of the Pauline doctrine of justification.[34]

In order to interpret justification by faith, the Pauline writings on this subject must be in its proper contextual setting, its *Sitz im Leben*.[35] Paul is writing from a first-century

30. Wright, *What Saint Paul Really Said*, 245.
31. Wright, *Paul*, 122.
32. Wright, *Justification*, 117–18.
33. Wright, *Paul*, 111–12.
34. Ibid., 113.
35. *Sitz im Leben*, used in form criticism, seeks to place Scripture

Deficiencies in the Justification of the Ungodly

Jewish perspective to first-century Jews. These Jews are not seeking to gain salvation (i.e., entrance into God's covenant family) but rather to demonstrate their membership through works.[36] Justification by faith *alone* is misleading. The actual phrase "justification by faith alone" gives the appearance that faith and works are "mutually exclusive."[37] For first-century Jews, covenant language regarding works—more specifically, works of the Torah—calls to mind the blessings and curses that come from obedience. The blessings and curses that come from obedience are not in the sense of losing one's salvation, but rather in the sense of being obedient to God and demonstrating this obedience through works.[38]

Justification by faith, as William Wrede and Albert Schweitzer assert, is a Pauline parenthetical theological argument for the inclusion of Gentiles into God's covenant family.[39] Schweitzer further affirms that justification by faith holds a secondary role to Paul's main point, which is about the person of Christ and the gospel message.[40] While Schweitzer's assessment that justification by faith plays a secondary role is questionable, he correctly identifies the inseparability of justification by faith and the message of the gospel. Nevertheless, justification is not the central theme of the Pauline letters.[41] The central theme of the Pauline letters, particularly in the Epistle to the Romans, is

---

in its proper "original life setting" (Elwell and Yarbrough, *Encountering*, 172).

36. Wright, *Paul*, 113–20.

37. Wright, *Climax*, 6.

38. Ibid., 142.

39. Wright, *Justification*, 84–85.

40. Schweitzer, *Mysticism of Paul*, 225; Wright, *What Saint Paul Really Said*, 113–14.

41. Wright, *What Saint Paul Really Said*, 114–15.

the "salvation-history" of the Jews and Gentiles, primarily found in chapters 9–11.[42]

Justification by faith means that all who are in God's covenant family are one in Christ. All who believe, including the Gentiles, are members of God's family baptized as one into Christ and are therefore heirs to the promises given to Abraham. The fulfillment of the promises through the work of the Messiah now includes both Jews and Gentiles based on the verdict of righteousness from God for those justified by faith.[43] In essence, as Stendahl clearly states, Paul is making a "scriptural argument, according to the exegetical principles of Judaism,"[44] for the inclusion of the Gentiles into the covenant family of God through justification by faith.

Imputed Righteousness

The traditional view of imputed righteousness, according to Wright, holds similar shortcomings and misinterpretations, as does the traditional view of justification. Imputed righteousness has to do with a *declaration* of righteousness that places the believer in *right* covenant standing with God. God's righteousness, particularly in regards to saving the world, has to do with his covenant faithfulness to Israel. Therefore, imputed righteousness is a *right* status declaration for covenant membership. For Gentile believers, this is a declaration of an ecclesiastical membership with the Jews in God's single family.[45] The church is now a part of God's covenant membership in an ecclesiastical setting because

---

42. Wright, "Paul of History," 62; Wright, *Justification*, 35, 131.
43. Wright, *Justification*, 131, 134.
44. Stendahl, "Judaism and Christianity," 6.
45. Wright, *What Saint Paul Really Said*, 134–35.

Deficiencies in the Justification of the Ungodly

through Christ Jews and Gentiles are now a part of God's single family.[46] There are three main components to the doctrine of imputed righteousness: *covenant, law court,* and *eschatology.*

Covenant

First, the view of imputed righteousness holds a *covenant* emphasis. The word *righteousness* means the righteousness of God; it does not mean the righteousness of humanity. In regard to justification, God's righteousness has to do with his own righteousness as it pertains to his *covenant* faithfulness with Israel. God's righteousness stands firm despite Israel's *covenant* unfaithfulness. God is righteous and trustworthy in keeping his covenant promises with Israel for salvation.[47]

In the OT, Israel makes an appeal to God's righteousness for release from her Babylonian exile.[48] God's righteousness and faithfulness prevails as he grants Israel mercy by releasing her from her captors. The righteousness of God is an attribute or characteristic of God and is prevalent in his covenant faithfulness to Israel.

The traditional NT interpretation of God's righteousness is incorrect because it does not take into consideration the view of a first-century Jew.[49] God's righteousness relates to his faithfulness in fulfilling his covenant promises. God imputes his faithfulness to Israel as a *covenant* keeper. He does not give Israel his righteousness. In other words, he

---

46. Wright, *Justification*, 99, 112, 116.
47. Wright, *What Saint Paul Really Said*, 96.
48. Wright, *Justification*, 63.
49. Ibid., 40.

does not transfer a physical object, substance or virtue to Israel.[50]

Law Court

Next, the view of imputed righteousness holds a *law court* emphasis. Imputed righteousness, as tradition affirms, refers to God's declaration of righteousness in forensic terms; however, tradition holds a misunderstanding of its declared consequence. The words *righteous* and *righteousness* are judicial court terms. The best explanation of the law court forensic setting for the declaration of imputed righteousness comes in a law court scenario.

In this law court scenario there is a judge (God), a plaintiff, and a defendant. The plaintiff is the accuser, and the defendant is the accused. For the Judge, righteousness means he will execute his judicial duties in accordance to the law, rendering a just verdict. He is an unbiased participant in the proceedings, punishing sin and the ungodly according to the law, therefore upholding justice for all, including the vulnerable and powerless. For the plaintiff or defendant, righteousness has a different meaning. Righteous has to do with the declaration or decision of the court. If the Judge rules in favor of the defendant, then the defendant is in right standing before the court. The same goes if the Judge rules in favor of the plaintiff.[51]

Therefore, imputed righteousness has to do with God's declarative verdict in favor of the defendant or the plaintiff announcing right standing before God. The Judge does not impart himself to the plaintiff or defendant; rather, he decrees a righteous verdict. The righteous verdict does

50. Wright, *What Saint Paul Really Said*, 98–99.
51. Ibid., 96–99.

Deficiencies in the Justification of the Ungodly

not make the beneficiary morally pure and upright. Rather, it is a vindication of the accusation against the defendant or in favor of the plaintiff.[52]

As the scenario shows, imputed righteousness is not a declaration of Christ's righteousness credited to believers in faith. The forensic language used in the Pauline writings regarding justification has to do with God's covenant faithfulness that returns order back into the universe through the judgment of God.[53] There is no *treasury* built up of Christ's *merits* for the credit of believers.[54]

Eschatology

Finally, the view of imputed righteousness holds an *eschatological* emphasis. Justification by faith invokes the eschatology of righteousness. Jews whom God will vindicate in the final judgment demonstrate their righteous standing through the works of the law. The declaration of the Jews as God's covenant people will come to pass in the eschaton. For the Jews, works of the law do not earn salvation but rather are a contemporary demonstration of their faith as God's covenant family. Works of the law are their badge, their boundary marker and identifier as members of the covenant family in their contemporary time and for the eschatological judgment to come.[55] Justification by faith

---

52. Ibid.

53. Wright, *What Saint Paul Really Said*, 117.

54. Wright, *Justification*, 134–35, 228, 231. In regard to merit, Wright is insinuating what he claims is a Protestant Reformed belief that Christ obeyed the law perfectly thereby building a treasury of merit that is then reckoned to believers. The use of the phrase *treasury of merit* also makes the comparison to the Roman Catholic view of indulgences (Hardon, *Catholic Catechism*, 560–62).

55. Wright, *What Saint Paul Really Said*, 99, 118.

compares in the Pauline writings to works of the law in the OT, in that faith is now the boundary marker, the badge, demonstrated by God's people (both Jews and Gentiles). Faith is a contemporary event followed by an end-time judgment.[56] In essence, the process of justification denotes a past, present, and future judgment.

The eschatological judgment in the Pauline writings on justification by faith does not eliminate good works, such as obedience, morality, and good behavior. These works are a part of God's future judgment because "justification by faith is what happens in the *present time*, anticipating the verdict of the *future day* when God judges the world."[57] The Pauline writings declare a final and future judgment before the judgment seat of Christ for all humanity including God's people. Justification by faith, from an eschatological viewpoint, has to do with works.[58] Justification in the present time is by faith and a public life of obedience. Good works attest to a future, eschatological justification.[59] The NT person now lives between the judgment of sin in the death and resurrection of Jesus Christ and the final judgment in the eschaton. God's covenant people now live and die for God (Rom 14:8), and everything that God's people do between now and the eschaton will come to account in the final judgment.[60]

---

56. Wright, *Paul*, 120–21.

57. Wright, *Surprised*, 139–40; Wright, *What Saint Paul Really Said*, 118–19, 131–32.

58. Wright, *Surprised*, 139.

59. Wright, *What Saint Paul Really Said*, 129.

60. Wright, *Romans Part 2*, 103–4.

Deficiencies in the Justification of the Ungodly

Philippians 3:9 and 2 Corinthians 5:20–21

As further evidence of the misinterpretation of imputed righteousness, two passages come to mind: Philippians 3:9 and 2 Corinthians 5:20–21. The Reformed view mistakenly interprets the phrase *dikaisosyne theou* to mean that God imputes his righteousness. This phrase has to do with the Creator God's responsibility or obligation to reconcile the world in righteousness by being faithful to his covenant promises.[61] Philippians 3:9 and 2 Corinthians 5:20–21 both demonstrate the use of God's righteousness *dikaisosyne theou* in the Pauline letters. The translation of Philippians 3:9 is as follows.

> [A]nd be found in him, not having a righteousness of my own that comes from the law, but one that comes through faith in Christ, the righteousness from God based on faith.[62]

The passage starts with the translation of the phrase "faith in Christ" to mean *the faithfulness of Christ*. It then continues with the key phrase, which "is not *dikaisosyne theou*, 'God's righteousness,' but *dikaiosune ek theou*, righteousness *from* God."[63] The righteousness referred to in this verse has to do with a declarative status only. This references the Hebrew law court, where the Judge (God) declares the defendant (Israel) in right covenant standing. God does not give the defendant his righteousness. The phrase "be found in him [Christ]"[64] in 3:9a has to do with the covenant family's sharing in the suffering, death, and resurrection of

---

61. Wright, *Paul*, 25–26.

62. Wright, *What Saint Paul Really Said*, 104. This is Wright's translation of the verse.

63. Ibid.

64. Wright, *Climax*, 48; Wright, *Resurrection*, 305.

N. T. Wright

Christ, thereby receiving a righteous declaration that is not their own.[65] This covenantal status belongs to those who are in Christ and comes from God's declaration.[66] For Paul, it is about a status—a declared covenant status that comes from being in Christ. In the passage, Paul contrasts the righteousness of keeping Torah to the righteousness that comes from the status of being in Christ.[67] It is this declarative status that is the "great Pauline truth to which the sub-Pauline idea of 'the imputation of Christ's righteousness' is truly pointing."[68]

In 2 Corinthians 5:20–21, Paul writes about his ministry as an apostle. The translation of the two verses is as follows:

> We are ambassadors for Christ, as though God were making his appeal through us. We appeal on behalf of Christ, 'be reconciled to God.' God made him to be sin for us, who knew no sin, so that in him we might become the *dikaiosune theou*.[69]

In this passage, traditional theological exegetes correctly translate *dikaisosyne theou* in its proper context to mean *the righteousness of God*. However, the traditional belief that the primary meaning of the passage has to do with justification is incorrect. Rather, Paul is discussing his ministry as an apostle.[70]

---

65. Ibid.
66. Wright, *Climax*, 48.
67. Wright, *Prison Letters*, 119–20.
68. Wright, *Justification*, 141–42.
69. Wright, *What Saint Paul Really Said*, 104. This is Wright's translation of the verses.
70. Ibid.

Deficiencies in the Justification of the Ungodly

The passage details the reconciliation of the world to God through Jesus Christ the Messiah, a rescue operation from God to humanity.[71] All who are therefore in Christ are new creations in a new world. The new King of the new world is Jesus Christ. His ambassadors are the apostles, who proclaim a ministry of reconciliation through the gospel.[72] As ambassadors of Christ, the apostles are a part of the new covenant ministry, "an incarnation of the covenant faithfulness of God."[73]

Because of the reconciling work of Christ, the apostles and all who believe are now in Christ. They are now ambassadors who are a part of God's covenant righteousness. In other words, they are the embodiment of the righteousness of God in that they are in Christ, sharing in his death and resurrection so that they now share in his suffering.[74]

The notion that verse 21 refers to an imputed righteousness that comes from Christ is mistaken. Such a notion is out of context with the rest of the chapter and appears out of step with the primary message of the passage. This is the result of the overemphasis of a doctrine that is not actually stated per se in the Pauline writings. Contemporary theologians such as John Piper commit these types of hermeneutical mistakes by relying only on the narrow writings of traditional scholars such as John Calvin and the authors of the Westminster Confession. When theologians such as Piper reach for tradition rather than the Bible for answers to theological questions (e.g., imputed righteousness), hermeneutical mistakes inevitably occur.[75]

---

71. Wright, *After You Believe*, 129.

72. Wright, *2 Corinthians*, 62–67.

73. Wright, *Paul Really Said*, 104–5.

74. Wright, *Resurrection*, 304–05; Wright, *Climax*, 48.

75. Wright, *What Saint Paul Really Said*, 105; Wright, *Justification*, 44–46, 105, 163–65.

N. T. Wright

While the systematic theological debate continues regarding imputed righteousness, the actual phrase "the imputed righteousness of Christ" is not in the Pauline writings. The writings of two traditional theologians, Michael Bird and J. I. Packer, both allude in their respective writings that the essence of the imputation of Christ's righteousness does exist in the Pauline epistles; however, the actual phrase does not exist.[76]

In closing, while examining Wright's view of imputed righteousness, it is worth noting that Wright believes that Christ bore the sins of the many, which is the imputation of sins to Christ from sinners.[77] However, he does not believe in the imputation of the righteousness of Christ to sinners. An examination of this discrepancy is forthcoming in this book.

---

76. Ibid., 46; Bird, *Saving Righteousness of God*, 70, 87; Packer, "Justification," 685.

77. Wright, *Justification*, 136.

3

The Traditional View of Imputed Righteousness

JUSTIFICATION

The next step in evaluating Wright's view of imputed righteousness is to gain a clearer understanding of the traditional Protestant Reformed view as it currently stands. Evaluating Wright's view begins by examining how the early church fathers struggled and dealt with this doctrine in the past, and then looking at how this doctrine developed to become the traditional view. Gaining a clearer understanding of the traditional view of imputed righteousness will help address the many dogmatic caricatures lodged against the traditional view by Wright.[1]

---

1. Wright has the tendency to make dogmatic caricatures against alleged beliefs and views of the traditional view of justification, including the traditional view of imputed righteousness, throughout his writings. Unfortunately, there are no citation references given for many of his caricatures for further examination. Wright's caricatures

The Traditional View of Imputed Righteousness

In Christianity, the doctrine of justification is central to the teaching of God's reconciliation with the ungodly sinner through the work of Jesus Christ. Assurance of salvation from eternal damnation comes from understanding the justifying work of Christ.[2] Alister McGrath calls the assurance of salvation the "essence of the Christian faith."[3] In Pauline theology, there is an inevitable connection between justification and God's righteousness. More specifically, the doctrine of justification does not exist without the righteousness of God.[4]

In traditional theology, salvation through the justifying work of Christ involves God's call through the proclamation of the gospel message. The gospel calls the ungodly to trust in Jesus Christ. The ungodly cannot effectually respond to God's call through the gospel message without the work of the Holy Spirit in regeneration.[5] Regeneration occurs when God bestows a new life onto the ungodly.[6] Conversion then occurs when the newborn Christian responds to the gospel message through repentance and faith

---

give the false impression that what he has stated is unquestionably traditional dogma. For example, regarding imputed righteous, Wright states, "Righteousness is not an object, a substance or a gas which can be passed across the courtroom" (Wright, *What Saint Paul Really Said*, 98). Wright also states, "Here we meet, not for the last time, the confusion that arises inevitably when we try to think of the judge transferring, by imputation or any other way, his own attributes to the defendant" (Wright, *Justification*, 66).

2. Luther, *Galatians*, 66–67; McGrath, *Luther's Theology*, 8. Christians faithfully seek this assurance through their understanding of the doctrine of justification.

3. McGrath, *Luther's Theology*, 8.

4. Garlington, "Justification by Faith," 58.

5. Augustine, *Galatians*, 157.

6. Hoekema, *God's Image*, 8.

Deficiencies in the Justification of the Ungodly

in Jesus Christ. Regeneration is a creative act by God unto the humans who passively receives it.[7]

The next step in the process of salvation comes with God's response to the newborn Christian's faith in Christ by fulfilling his promise of forgiving sin and thereby removing guilt. This is a declarative act whereby God forgives sin and any liability that goes with it.[8] This process of salvation involves the sinner's response to God's effectual calling, "Those whom he called he also justified (Rom 8:30), which brings the sinner in union with Christ."[9] Traditional theologians associated justification, including imputed righteousness, with God's redemptive work, sometimes referred to as *the golden chain*[10]—"whom He predestined, these He also called; whom He called, these He also justified; and whom He justified, these He also glorified."[11] Justification, in this golden chain, is the act of God wherein he pardons the sins of the ungodly and accepts them as righteous.[12] The pardoning of sins comes through justification by the atoning work of Jesus Christ. Christ removes the curse of sin all for God's glory.[13] This righteousness spoken about is a judicial or forensic declarative pronouncement given by God to the ungodly sinner who receives it by faith alone. The act of imputed righteousness is a declarative pronouncement that does not make sinners upright, righteous, or holy. Rather, it is a declaration by God (the Judge) in favor of the ungodly whereby the ungodly sinner receives credit for Christ's

---

7. Berkhof, *Systematic Theology*, 465.
8. Grudem, *Systematic Theology*, 722.
9. Hodge, *Romans*, 286.
10. Ibid.; Williamson, *Westminster Confession*, 136.
11. Williamson, *Westminster Confession*, 136; Rom 8:30.
12. Westminster Confession, 376.
13. Calvin, *Romans*, 139–41; Rom 3:24–25; 4:25.

The Traditional View of Imputed Righteousness

redemptive work.[14] Theologian Millard J. Erickson writes, "The imputation of Christ's righteousness is not, then, so much a matter of transferring something from him [Christ] to me, as it is of bringing the two of us together so that we hold all things in common."[15]

Traditional theologians, such as Luther, Calvin, Murray, Williamson, and Hoekema, understand the implication of imputed righteousness as Christ's righteousness imputed, credited, or reckoned to an ungodly person by faith. Thus, God justifies the ungodly believer by reckoning Christ's righteousness on his/her behalf.[16] The basis of this theological understanding comes from the Pauline corpus of work found in Holy Scripture.[17] A traditional understanding of the doctrine of justification, including the imputation of righteousness, begins with the Old Testament and continues with final clarity in the New Testament. The development of this doctrine is not something that happened overnight. God's salvation plan for humanity begins in the Old Testament and comes to fruition in the New Testament with the coming of the Messiah. The New Testament, particularly the Pauline writings, fully reveals God's salvific plan, which includes the justification of the ungodly by the imputation of Christ's righteousness. The church fathers' struggle with the doctrine of justification, including the imputation of righteousness, led to a division in the church (Protestant/Roman Catholic), and today's traditional view of justification is the result of this struggle.

Wright disagrees with this view of justification and imputed righteousness. Wright does not believe that Christ

14. Murray, *Redemption*, 50–51.
15. Erickson, *Christian Doctrine*, 264.
16. Murray, *Redemption*, 124–25.
17. Ibid.; Westminster Confession, 50–51; Williamson, *Westminster Confession*, 138; Rom 3:22–28; 4:3, 5–7; 5:17–19; 2 Cor 5:19, 21.

imputes his righteousness to the sinner. He does not believe that the declaration of righteousness reckons anything to the sinner for salvation (soteriology).[18] Rather, he believes that the declaration is only a pronouncement that the sinner is now in "right" covenant standing within God's family. His view does not deal with a forgiven sinner's righteous standing before God, but rather it deals with a covenant member's right standing in relationship to another covenant member.[19]

Again, Wright's view of the doctrine of imputed righteousness is subtle and theologically different from the traditional Reformed view. Wright does not believe that justification through the declaration of righteousness imputed to the ungodly sinner is salvific in terms of receiving credit for Christ's obedience unto death (soteriology).[20] Rather, he believes that the declaration of righteousness places the covenant member back in right covenant standing and is thereby salvific (ecclesiology).[21] However, he makes no allowances for any exchange between the sinner and the righteous obedience of Christ. Further, Wright does not believe that the gospel message in the Pauline writings has anything to do with how people receive salvation or how someone becomes a Christian. Rather, Wright believes that the gospel message in the Pauline writings has to do with "the proclamation of the Lordship of Jesus Christ."[22]

---

18. Wright, *What Saint Paul Really Said*, 96–99, 117.

19. Horton, "Soteriology and Ecclesiology."

20. Wright, *Justification*, 134–35.

21. Wright, *What Saint Paul Really Said*, 119; Wright, *Justification*, 242.

22. Ibid., *What Saint Paul Really Said*, 60, 90, 125, 132–33, 153.

The Traditional View of Imputed Righteousness

Imputation

Before continuing the study of justification, one must first gain a better understanding of the biblical meaning of *imputation*. The effects of imputation on posterity appear evident in three primary ways. Benjamin Warfield refers to the effects of imputation as the *Three Acts of Imputation*.[23] These acts are, "the imputation of Adam's sin to his posterity; the imputation of the sins of his people to the Redeemer; [and] the imputation of the righteousness of Christ to His people."[24] The full development and application of the term imputation came about during and shortly after the Reformation period.[25] The word imputation is a forensic word used in a law court setting. It can mean to reckon, as in, "to reckon something to someone's account."[26] Hodges refers to the term as "familiar and unambiguous."[27] The term can also mean to credit or debit someone's account. Paul tells Onesimus regarding Philemon in verse 18, "If he has wronged you in any way, or owes you anything, charge that to my account." The Greek word *logizesthai* comes from the Latin Vulgate verb *imputo*. The use of the verb *imputo* derives from a bookkeeping/accounting metaphor (e.g., credited, accounted, reckoned, and imputed) and can be applicable in a forensic setting.[28] Other verses that use the term imputed or convey the meaning of imputation are 1 Sam 22:15; 2 Sam 19:19; Lev 7:18, 17:4; Ps 32:2; Rom 4:6; and 2 Cor 5:19.[29]

23. Warfield, *Theology*, 302.
24. Ibid.
25. Ibid.
26. Hoekema, *God's Image*, 156.
27. Hodge, *Systematic Theology*, 144.
28. Warfield, *Theology*, 301.
29. Hodge, *Systematic Theology*, 144.

Deficiencies in the Justification of the Ungodly

The Imputation of Adam's Sin to Posterity

While there is no direct mention in the Bible of the imputation of Adam's sin onto posterity, there is a manifestation of its biblical meaning. This is to say that the guilt for Adam's sin affects his posterity as a judgment upon humanity. Adam is the head and first of all sinners in the entire human race. It is through Adam that sin comes into the world.[30] Some theologians throughout Christian history, such as Augustine and Hodge, refer to Adam's sin as *original sin*; however, this term is misleading because it gives the impression that it is Adam's first sin rather than the guilt of posterity's sin. Grudem prefers to call this act "inherited sin."[31] God views the guilt of Adam's sinful transgression as posterity's transgression. Being guilty of transgressing the law imputes sin to the guilty party, and from sin comes death to all who sin.[32] Paul writes in Romans 5:12, "Therefore, just as sin came into the world through one man, and death came through sin, and so death spread to all because all have sinned." The imputation of Adam's sin to posterity could not exist if there were no connection between Adam and posterity. Therefore, "As he fell from the estate in which he was created, they [posterity] fell with him in his first transgression, so that the penalty of that sin came upon them as well as upon him."[33] The epistle to the Romans affirms the imputation of

30. Morris, *Romans*, 227–28.

31. Grudem, *Systematic Theology*, 494.

32. Murray, *Adam's Sin*, 71–72.

33. Hodge, *Systematic Theology*, 196. In the fifth century AD, a British Monk named Pelagius and his followers denied any connection between Adam's sin and the sins of his posterity. Pelagius believed that Adam and his posterity were/are born in a neutral state, being neither good nor bad. This belief later became known as Pelagianism. The Councils of Carthage and Ephesus later condemned this belief as heresy. Cf. McGrath, *Historical Theology*, 79–81; Hoekema, *God's*

The Traditional View of Imputed Righteousness

Adam's sin to his posterity in verse 5:19, "For just as by the one man's disobedience the many were made sinners, so by the one man's obedience the many will be made righteous." *Imputation* is the technical term for the bestowment of the guilt of Adam's sin onto posterity.[34] Therefore, the need for salvation upon God's covenant people comes through the redemptive work of Christ.[35] Wright acknowledges that the sin of Adam curses the entire world. Further, he affirms that the nation of Israel was in Adam and that both failed on God's single plan for the world. Israel repeats the sin of Adam by rebelling against God.[36]

The Imputation of Sin to Christ

The imputation of sin to Christ brings atonement to his covenant people. The righteousness of God demands the punishment of sin, which means the punishment of the sinner.[37] The Old Testament demonstrates this truth in the Jewish sacrificial system, which is an expiatory system with reference to the removal of sin and guilt from the ungodly. The sacrificial substitutionary blood offering of an animal in place of the ungodly sinner covers the sins and withholds the wrath of God. In this system, an exchange between the sinner and the sacrificial animal takes place prior to the sacrifice. A symbolic transfer of the worshiper's sins onto the animal occurs by the laying on of the sinner's hands on the head of the animal.[38] In essence, the ungodly sinner is

---

Image, 154–56.

34. Luther, *Romans*, 77–79.
35. Grudem, *Systematic Theology*, 495.
36. Wright, *Justification*, 99, 196, 241.
37. Luther, *Romans*, 78; Deut 24:16.
38. Murray, *Redemption*, 24–25.

Deficiencies in the Justification of the Ungodly

imputing his sins onto the sacrificial animal. This is a foreshadowing of the ultimate sacrifice yet to come. In the New Testament, Jesus Christ pays the penalty for the sins of the elect. God imputes sin onto Christ for the atonement of his covenant people.

The Pauline writings explicitly describe the sacrificial atoning work of Jesus Christ on the cross, and they clearly describe the imputation of sin onto Christ. Paul writes in 2 Corinthians 5:21, "For our sake he made him to be sin who knew no sin, so that in him we might become the righteousness of God."[39] Further, the language used by Paul is clearly covenant language, although the actual use of the word "covenant" by Paul is infrequent.[40] The New Testament clearly views Jesus Christ as the sacrificial Lamb of God who will take away the sins of the world. This is reminiscent of Genesis 22: the command to sacrifice Isaac. When Isaac questions his father about the lack of the sacrificial animal, Abraham tells Isaac that God will provide the sacrifice. This story holds significance to Christians who know that God did provide the true sacrificial Lamb of God. The binding of Isaac holds significance to Jews who relate to Isaac's willingness to go along with his father's plan.[41] The Pauline writings repeatedly mention that Christ died for humanity and that Christ died for sin. Examples of Pauline verses relating to the imputation of sin to Christ are as follows: Romans 4:25, "who [Christ] was handed over to death for our trespasses and was raised for our justification"; 1 Corinthians 15:3, 5 ". . . that Christ died for our sins in accordance with the scripture, and that he appeared to Cephas, then to the twelve"; Galatians 1:4, "who [Christ] gave himself for our sins to set us free from the present evil age . . ."; Romans

39. Morris, *Romans*, 191.
40. Williams, *Far as the Curse*, 226.
41. Morris, *Preaching of the Cross*, 139.

The Traditional View of Imputed Righteousness

6:10, "The death he died, he [Christ] died to sin"; Romans 5:6, "for while we were still weak, at the right time Christ died for the ungodly"; and Romans 5:8, "But God proves his love for us in that while we still were sinners Christ died for us."[42] Ultimately, Christ is the propitiation of the sins imputed to him by God on behalf of his covenant people. Christ turns away God's wrath by paying the penalty for sin. Christ's act of propitiation is his personal action affecting God's covenant people in an extremely personal way.[43]

Wright clearly acknowledges that God deals with the sin of the world through the death of Jesus Christ on the cross. He refers to Christ as Israel's representative, who through his faithfulness was their substitutionary atonement.[44] By this acknowledgement, Wright is therefore admitting that Israel (God's covenant family) is the beneficiary of Christ's redemptive work and is receiving some type of credit on their behalf.

The Imputation of Christ's Righteousness to the Ungodly

Holy Scripture goes to great lengths to condemn unrighteousness and acknowledge righteousness. Moreover, the biblical writers, in both Old and New Testaments, condemn those who declare an unrighteous person righteous and a righteous person unrighteous. God, who is by nature the definition of justice, does not deviate from divine truth in his justification of the ungodly.[45] *Justification* is a judicial term that depicts a declarative pronouncement from the

42. Morris, *Cross*, 217.

43. Morris, *Atonement*, 151–52.

44. Wright, *Justification*, 207; Wright, *What Saint Paul Really Said*, 106–07.

45. Murray, *Redemption*, 123.

Deficiencies in the Justification of the Ungodly

Judge (God). This occurs when the Judge declares a person righteous by the merit of the law. The Judge simply weighs the evidence and announces his findings. It is "not" a declaration whereby the Judge overlooks the guilt of the accused and places the person in right covenant standing.[46] For humanity, acquittal is impossible; they stand convicted and condemned. Justification can only occur with the imputation of the righteousness of Christ to the ungodly. Christ who knew no sin became sin for the forgiveness and eternal life of God's covenant people.[47] The righteousness of Christ is more than just the forgiveness of sin. It encompasses his perfect obedience, both passive and active. His passive obedience on the cross pays the penalty for sin. His active obedience executes perfectly the demands of the law placed upon humanity.[48] God imputes Christ's righteousness, which is an alien righteousness[49] to the ungodly. Therefore, without violating his own just nature, God regards the ungodly as righteous.[50] Further, this righteousness comes not through the works of the ungodly but through faith in the justifying work of Christ. Even the faith required for

---

46. Ibid., 122.

47. Berkhof, *Systematic Theology*, 523. As taught, according to Berkhof, in many scriptural passages, including Rom 3:24; 5:9, 19; 8:1; 10:4; 1 Cor 1:30; 6:11; 2 Cor 5:21; Phil 3:9.

48. Ritschl, *Justification and Reconciliation*, 66.

49. Luther, *Galatians*, 98–101; Mannermaa, *Christ Present in Faith*, 26; Seifrid, "Righteousness Language," 70–71. The term *alien righteousness* comes from Martin Luther. This is a righteousness that does not originate in the ungodly sinner but comes externally; it is alien to the sinner. This righteousness is the union of Christ with the sinner whereby Christ's righteousness belongs to the sinner and the sins of the ungodly belong to Christ.

50. Williamson, *Westminster Confession*, 138.

The Traditional View of Imputed Righteousness

justification is a gift from God. Therefore, justification is the gift of grace from God.[51]

The term *justification by faith* is not referring to the faithfulness of Christ (although he is faithful *par excellence*), but rather it refers to faith in Christ.[52] Therefore, the imputation of righteousness involves what Luther calls the "blessed exchange between Christ and the sinner"[53] whereby through faith in Christ an exchange occurs between the sins of the ungodly and the righteousness of Christ. Christ and the forgiven sinner become one.[54] Grudem writes, "When we say that God *imputes* Christ's righteousness to us it means that God *thinks of* Christ's righteousness as belonging to us, or regards it as *belonging* to us."[55]

Wright disagrees with this view of imputed righteousness. He does not believe that God's declaration imputes the righteousness of Christ to the ungodly. He does not believe that the ungodly receive credit imputed to them by faith for Christ obedience on the cross.[56] He calls this a category mistake. Rather, he believes that the declaration of righteousness places the covenant member back in right covenant standing.[57] He makes no allowances for any ex-

51. Westminster Confession, 208–9.

52. Seifrid, *Christ*, 139–40. Siefred addresses the debate regarding whether or not the genitive denotes the object, as in *faith in Christ*, or the genitive, denoting the subject as in *Christ's faith(fulness)*. The earliest Christians, according to Seifred, understood "justification by faith" to mean *by faith in Christ* not *by the faithfulness of Christ*. Further, New Testament writers convey the message that belief in Christ brings salvation.

53. Luther, *Luther's Works*, 316; Seifrid, "Righteousness Language," 71.

54. Ibid.; Althaus, *Martin Luther*, 213.

55. Grudem, *Systematic Theology*, 726.

56. Wright, *Justification*, 134–35.

57. Wright, *What Saint Paul Really Said*, 119; Wright, *Justification*,

change between the sinner and the righteous obedience of Christ unto death.

Old Testament

When examining the word justification in the Pauline writings, it is of the utmost importance to identify the methodology used by Paul to write his epistles. Although, the Pauline writings may indicate Paul's Hellenistic influences and a familiarity with the mystery religions, the epistles also indicate that the apostle based his writings on an exegetical study of the Old Testament writings themselves.[58] The concepts of justice, justification, and righteousness are not inventions from the mind of Paul but rather find their bases in the Old Testament.[59]

Examining the terms used in the Old Testament for the words "justification" and "righteousness," the Greek word *dikaioō* appears most often in the Septuagint and means to *declare* or *make righteous*.[60] In the Hebrew Bible, the word *tsadaq*, which can mean *righteous*, *just*, or *to make just*, appears in a number of passages.[61] However, the term *hitsdik*, which means *to justify*, appears a greater number of times than does the term *tsadaq*.[62] A better translation for

---

232, 242.

58. Barth, *Justification*, 14–15.

59. Ibid. According to Barth, the Old Testament texts used by Paul are different from those used today. These texts, however, are close enough to make a study of Paul's observational use of the Old Testament. On several occasions, Paul uses the Greek version of the Hebrew texts. At times, he uses the LXX text rather than the Hebrew (Morris, *Romans*, 193).

60. Barth, *Justification*, 15.

61. Meeks, *Christian Theology*, 419–20.

62. Berkhof, *Systematic Theology*, 510.

The Traditional View of Imputed Righteousness

the term *hitsdik* is "to declare judicially that one's state is in harmony with the demands of the law."[63] The terms refer to the standards needed for being in *right* accord with God and the law.[64] The Old Testament use of this term (*hitsdik*) is in the verb context. This indicates that it is only through God's declarative action that a person can come into righteous harmony with God. This is to say that God takes the action needed for righteousness.[65] The terms used to define the Old Testament meaning of justification and righteousness are forensic terms. This is to say that these terms are legalistic terms used in a law court setting.[66] Further, these terms are in direct contrast with the terms used for condemnation (e.g., Deut 25:1; Prov 17:15; Isa 5:23). This assures its legalistic reference rather than a moralistic connotation the indication of which means judgment.[67] The severe result of being out of harmony with God is eternal condemnation.

God's action in justification is an action whereby God imputes (reckons/credits) righteousness to the ungodly. God's favor upon the sinner imputes righteous harmony for his/her justification. In Psalm 106:28–31, Phinehas' zealous action against idolatry finds favor with God. Phinehas believes and obeys God, and God reckons (credits/imputes) it as righteousness. It is this righteousness, on Phineas' behalf, that atones from Israel's sinfulness by turning away God's wrath.[68] This act is certainly a foreshadowing of the Messiah still to come. In much the same way, Abraham's faith and obedience finds favor with God. Abraham "believed the

63. Ibid.

64. Meeks, *Christian Theology*, 420.

65. McGrath, "Justification," 518.

66. Berkhof, *Systematic Theology*, 510.

67. Ibid.

68. VanLandingham, *Judgment & Justification*, 63; Kugel, *Bible as It Was*, 497; Num 25.

Deficiencies in the Justification of the Ungodly

LORD, and the LORD reckons it to him as righteousness" (Gen 15:6). Both Phinehas' and Abraham's faith find favor with God, and through forensic language; God's declarative decree reckons their faith as righteousness.[69] Furthermore, Abraham's belief in God's promise and his acknowledgment that God is holy affirms that he is an ungodly sinner justified by God.[70]

Early Church Fathers

Origen

Origen is one of the first church fathers to write about justification in his commentary to the Romans written between AD 244 and 246.[71] Origen for the most part mistakenly believes that justification is from God but requires the works of merit or demerit prior to God's final judgment. He believes that Paul's use of the phrase "justification by faith" is merely a figure of speech that encapsulates the idea of justification.[72] The grace of justification brings forgiveness for past sins. However, according to Origen, this forgiveness does not apply to future sins.[73]

Athanasius

Athanasius' role in the development of the doctrine of justification has to do with his writings on the incarnation of Christ. While still in his twenties, Athanasius' treatise

69. Kugel, *Bible as It Was*, 497.
70. Seifrid, *Christ*, 68.
71. Scheck, *Origen*, 13.
72. Ibid., 51–52.
73. Ibid., 35.

The Traditional View of Imputed Righteousness

entitled *De incarnatione* (On the Incarnation) defends the deity of Christ. His treatise had a major impact on Christians of his day and was instrumental during the Arian controversy.[74] He claims that if Christ is not fully God then redemption for humanity has not and cannot occur. He writes, "he by his own power demonstrates to be divine, subduing the pretensions of idols by his supposed humiliation—by the cross—and those who mock and disbelieve invisibly winning over to recognize his divinity and power."[75] Further, Athanasius states that if Christ is not God then Christians are idolaters.[76] Therefore, justification by God is "the redemption of the world by the incarnate Word."[77]

Saint Augustine

Saint Augustine's contributions to Christian theology are many. Augustine's writings on the doctrine of grace during the Pelagian controversy reflect his views of justification. In the fifth century, a British monk named Pelagius wrote about the ability of humans to initiate their own salvation through the obedience of the law. Pelagius' denies the need for God's grace in obtaining salvation.

Augustine emphatically denies Pelagius' claim citing the need for God's grace in every stage of the Christian's life from birth to death.[78] According to Augustine, fallen

---

74. Erickson, *Christian Doctrine*, 220–21. The Arian controversy questioned the deity of Jesus. It is later condemned as heresy at the Council of Nicea (AD 325). Arius believed that Christ was a created being. The status of Son comes from the Father, but Christ is not of the same nature (McGrath, *Historical Theology*, 49–51).

75. Athanasius, "Incarnation," 55.

76. McGrath, *Historical Theology*, 26.

77. Athanasius "Background and Ideas," 47.

78. Augustine, "De Natura et Gratia," 235–36; McGrath, *Historical*

Deficiencies in the Justification of the Ungodly

humanity does not possess the *freedom of the will* to do what is righteous and good but by nature only seek to do evil. It is because of this fallen nature that humanity cannot save itself.[79] Christians, according to Augustine, cannot fully observe the law without the grace of God. Augustine cites 2 Corinthians 3:6, "[God] who has made us competent to be ministers of a new covenant, not of letter but of spirit; for the letter kills, but the Spirit gives life." The letter is the law and the Spirit is the Holy Spirit.[80] Augustine also cites Romans 5:5[81] of which he states, "the love of God said to be poured out in our hearts is not that by which he loves us, but that by which he makes us love him." Augustine writes that God justifies sinners, "not that by which God is righteous, but that with which he clothes a human being when he justifies a sinner."[82] God clothes the sinner with righteousness for the forgiveness of sin and the justification of the ungodly. This is clearly a demonstration of an exchange between God and sinners.

Saint Anselm

Saint Anselm's part in dealing with the justification issue dealt with the question of how a holy and righteousness God can justify a sinner. Anselm believes that the basis of God's mercy is justice not according to merit but according to the

---

Theology, 35, 78–81.

79. McGrath, *Historical Theology*, 79–80; McGrath, *Iustitia Dei*, 25.

80. Heckel, "Is R. C. Sproul Wrong?," 94.

81. Rom 5:5: "and hope does not disappoint us, because God's love has been poured into our hearts through the Holy Spirit that has been given to us."

82. Augustine, "Spirit and the Letter," 9, 15, 32, 56; Heckel, "Is R. C. Sproul Wrong?," 94.

The Traditional View of Imputed Righteousness

highest good, *summum bonum*.[83] God seeks satisfaction for sin so that he can grant mercy. The price of sin against God is beyond any means or measures by which humanity can pay; hence, the answer to why God became man, *Cur Deus Homo*.[84] God's justice demands retribution for satisfaction of the sin committed against him by Adam and/or humanity. Humanity commits the injustice and humanity owes the penalty for the injustice.[85] However, the sin against God is such a grievous act that fallen tainted humanity cannot compensate the injustice.[86] It is Jesus Christ, the God-man, who makes satisfaction for the sins committed against God. It is through Christ that redemption comes to the ungodly by faith.[87]

Thomas Aquinas

Thomas Aquinas' view of justification is that God infuses grace upon a person thereby making that person just. Aquinas' magnum opus, the *Summa Theologiae*,[88] is perhaps his greatest and certainly among the most famous theological works of its time. His view of justification was the predominate view of the Roman Catholic Church during the Middle Ages, which later developed into a justification system of

---

83. McGrath, *Iustitia Dei*, 55.
84. Anselm, *Why God Became Man*.
85. Ibid., 67–68.
86. Ibid., 69–70.
87. McGrath, *Historical Theology*, 135–36.
88. Ibid., 136. The *Summa Theologiae*, which means "The Totality of Theology," is considered the greatest theology work during his contemporary middle ages.

merit.[89] According to Aquinas, justification is by God, but it is not just by faith alone.[90]

The Reformation

The development of the doctrine of justification just prior to the Reformation identifies justification with the sacrament of penance. It is not what Charles Carlson termed an "aberration of the nominalist theologians."[91] In other words, the doctrine of justification experiences a long period of growth during the middle ages prior to the Reformation. The growth is well within the accepted doctrinal structure of the church at that time.[92]

During the late middle ages just prior to the beginning of the Reformation, much confusion exist in the church regarding doctrinal issues, particularly the doctrine of justification. This confusion in large part was due to an exorbitant number of uneducated clergy who aggravated an already turbulent period in church history.[93] For the ungodly, the question of salvation was of vital concern. Therefore, the doctrine of justification through faith in Christ was of serious concern to those who sought assurance of their salvation. The reformers took the task of answering the question as to how salvation comes to the sinner. McGrath writes, "The practical importance of this question may be illustrated with reference to the fate of a small group of Italian noblemen at the beginning of the sixteenth century."[94]

---

89. Berkhof, *Systematic Theology*, 512.
90. Carlson, *Justification*, 119–20.
91. Ibid., 129.
92. Ibid.
93. McGrath, *Luther's Theology*, 8.
94. Ibid., 9.

The Traditional View of Imputed Righteousness

During the Reformation period, the greatest controversy for the reformers in the development of New Testament theology primarily involved the doctrine of justification. Attacks, arguments, and disagreements regarding this doctrine came from within and outside of reform circles.[95]

Martin Luther

During the late fourteenth and fifteenth centuries, many Christian philosophers come to accept a philosophical way of thinking termed *via moderna* (the modern way) as a way to study Scripture. Unfortunately, in regard to the doctrine of justification, this manner of philosophy leads to a very Pelagian way of thinking. This is the backdrop for much of Luther's writings on the doctrine of justification.[96] The influence of *via moderna* philosophy gives the appearance that justification comes from merit through works as an entitlement and not through the grace of God alone.[97] Luther, through his pursuit of divine truth regarding salvation, realizes that humanity is under the condemnation of God because of sin. He further realizes that *divine righteousness* demands divine wrath as punishment for sin and that no amount of works can merit justification. The only merit that a fallen human could earn is the merit of *perdition*.[98] The merit of perdition is the personal fear that Luther faces concerning his sins and the sins of humanity. This understanding of righteousness also brings terror to his heart when he prays Psalm 33:1, "... in your [God] righteousness deliver me." Luther stands convicted by his own

---

95. Chemnitz, *Justification*, 9.
96. McGrath, *Historical Theology*, 106–7.
97. Ibid., 119.
98. Kostlin, *Luther*, 72.

lack of righteousness. He later comes to realize through his study of Romans that the righteousness written of in Scripture is the righteousness that comes through faith, and the righteousness of the gospel.[99] Julius Kostlin writes that Luther now understands righteousness in the "passive sense, i.e., not as that by virtue of which God is righteous and condemns the ungodly, but as that with which God endows us, makes us righteous, justifies us—as a work wrought in us by God in his mercy."[100] Luther believes that the saving righteousness given by God through Jesus Christ to the ungodly is *iustitia aliena* (an alien righteousness). This is to say that God imputes this alien righteousness to the sinner by faith.[101] Luther writes,

> Believers inwardly are always sinners; therefore they are always justified from without. The hypocrites, (the work-righteous), on the other hand, are always righteous inwardly; therefore they are always sinners from without. By "inwardly" I mean, as we appear in our own judgment and opinion; by "from without," as we appear before God and his judgment. We are righteous "outside ourselves" when our righteousness does not flow from our works; but is ours alone by divine imputation.[102]

Philip Melanchthon

During the Reformation period, Melanchthon provided his Lutheran followers with a Christian document for which to

99. Ibid; McGrath, *Historical Theology*, 185–86.
100. Ibid.
101. McGrath, *Historical Theology*, 188.
102. Luther, *Romans*, 51.

The Traditional View of Imputed Righteousness

follow in living their daily lives entitled *Loci Communes*.[103] He developed many of Luther's ideas including Luther's view of justification by faith. In his writings, Melanchthon also develops the idea of a forensic justification whereby God declares and counts a believer as being righteous. He expounds upon Luther's idea of imputed righteousness.[104] McGrath believes that the developments by Melanchthon of church doctrines based on the Reformation movement mark a definite break away from the Roman Catholic Church and its religious dogma.[105] Attacks on Melanchthon's leadership came from both within Lutheran circles and outside Lutheranism centering on the doctrine of justification.[106]

John Calvin

John Calvin, one of the foremost theological scholars of the Reformation movement, gives finalization to the Protestant view of the doctrine of justification.[107] In 1551, the Osiandrian controversy brought about the development of the doctrine of justification whereby justification comes through the imputation the righteousness of Christ.[108] Calvin views justification by faith as the "principal point or the main hinge of the first part of this Epistle, that we are

---

103. McGrath, *Historical Theology*, 7.

104. Ibid., 189–90.

105. Ibid., 90.

106. Chemnitz, *Justification*, 9.

107. McCormack, "Justitia Aliena," 169–70.

108. McGrath, *Iustitia Dei*, 26–27. The Osiandrian controversy concerns the belief that Christ imparts his righteousness to the believer. Andreas Osiander, a Lutheran reformer, believed that saving righteousness came from Christ's divinity and was the indwelling of Christ (Wubbenhorst, "Calvin's Doctrine of Justification").

justified by faith through the mercy of God alone."[109] Calvin writes,

> [A] man will be justified by faith when, excluded from the righteousness of works, he by faith lays hold of the righteousness of Christ, and clothed in it appears in the sight of God not as a sinner, but as righteous. Thus we simply interpret justification as the acceptance with which God receives us into his favour as if we were righteous; and we say that this justification consists in the forgiveness of sins and the imputation of the righteousness of Christ.[110]

Calvin echoes and develops Luther's view of justification. He states that the sinner receives justification only through the righteousness of Christ, which God imputes to the sinner through faith.

The Heidelberg Catechism / The Westminster Confession of Faith and Catechism

The traditional Reformed view of the doctrines of justification and imputed righteousness continued to develop its orthodoxy after the Reformation, finding crystallization in church creeds and confessions. These confessions and statements include, but are not limited to, the Heidelberg Catechism and the Westminster Confession of Faith and Catechism.

In the Heidelberg Catechism, question 56 asks, "What do you believe concerning 'the forgiveness of sin?'" The catechism answers as follows:

---

109. Calvin, *Romans*, 66.
110. Calvin, "Mode of Obtaining," III, XI, 38.

The Traditional View of Imputed Righteousness

> I believe that God, because of Christ's atonement, will never hold against me any of my sins nor my sinful nature which I need to struggle against all my life. Rather, in grace God grants me the righteousness of Christ to free me forever from judgment.[111]

The Westminster Confession of Faith defines Justification as follows:

> Those whom God effectually calleth, he also freely justifieth: not by infusing righteousness into them, but by pardoning their sins, and by accounting and accepting their persons as righteous; not for anything wrought in them, or done by them, but for Christ's sake alone; nor by imputing faith itself, the act of believing, or any other evangelical obedience to them, as their righteousness; but by imputing the obedience and satisfaction of Christ unto them, they receiving and resting on him and his righteousness, by faith; which faith they have not of themselves, it is the gift of God.[112]

The doctrine of justification through the imputation of the righteousness of Christ developed over the course of many centuries. It encompasses an understanding of the righteousness of God and the fallen state of humanity. The teachings of this doctrine are central to a Christian's understanding of God's reconciliation with the ungodly.

---

111. Heidelberg Catechism, 32.
112. Westminster Confession, 50–51.

4

Critical Evaluation

A SUMMARY OF WRIGHT'S VIEW OF IMPUTED RIGHTEOUSNESS

THE FINAL STEP IN evaluating N. T. Wright's view of the doctrine of imputed righteousness is to examine where his view and the traditional Protestant Reformed view differ in theology. In brief, Wright does not believe that God's declaration imputes the righteousness of Christ, or anything else for that matter to the ungodly. Rather, the declarative pronouncement places the fallen or disobedience covenant member in right covenant standing based on God's covenant faithfulness. For Wright, the sinner (those in God's covenant family) makes an appeal to God, who renders a righteous decree in favor of his covenant people thereby placing them in right covenant standing.[1] Wright equates this forensic decree and covenant language

---

1. Wright, *What Saint Paul Really Said*, 96–99.

Critical Evaluation

to Daniel 9:7 and Deuteronomy 27-29. Because of her sinfulness, God is righteous in cursing Israel for violating her covenant with him and sending her into the Babylonian exile. Upon Israel's covenant appeal, God is righteous in blessing Israel by restoring her back in right covenant standing and thereby releasing her from her Babylonian exile.[2]

Further, according to Wright, justification is more about *ecclesiology* than *soteriology*. Wright does not believe that justification through the declaration of righteousness imputed to the ungodly sinner is salvific in terms of receiving credit for Christ obedience unto death (soteriology).[3] Rather, he believes that the declaration of righteousness places the covenant member back in right covenant standing and is thereby salvific (ecclesiology).[4] However, he makes no allowances for any exchange between the sinner and the righteous obedience of Christ. In fact, Wright does not believe that the gospel message in the Pauline writings has to do with how people receive salvation or how someone becomes a Christian. Rather, he believes that the gospel message in the Pauline writings has to do with "the proclamation of the Lordship of Jesus Christ."[5]

Wright rejects the notion that God (Christ) the Judge somehow transfers his righteousness to the ungodly, calling it a category mistake.[6] Justification is "not" about getting into the covenant family (i.e., salvation for the sinner). Rather, justification is about how to tell who is in the

2. Wright, *Justification*, 62-63.

3. Ibid., 134-35.

4. Wright, *What Saint Paul Really Said*, 119; Wright, *Justification*, 242.

5. Wright, *What Saint Paul Really Said*, 132-33.

6. Ibid.; cf. Wright, *Mark*, 233.

Deficiencies in the Justification of the Ungodly

covenant family.[7] God's righteousness has to do primarily with his faithful covenant relationship to Israel. Therefore, right standing in the covenant through faithful obedience is of the utmost importance in the declarative pronouncement.[8] Maintaining right standing in the covenant is the badge worn by God's covenant people. Justification is, therefore, about ecclesiology rather than soteriology. This is not the traditional Reformed view of imputed righteousness. Wright obfuscates his view by acknowledging that Christ bore the sins of the many, which is the imputation of sins to Christ,[9] while at the same time he rejects the imputation of Christ's righteousness to sinners for the justification of the ungodly.

AREAS OF DEFICIENCIES

The differences in Wright's view of the doctrine of imputed righteousness are subtle; however, major theological discrepancies do exist that are counter to the traditional Reformed view of Scripture. Research, based on the traditional Protestant Reformed view, reveals deficiencies in Wright's view of this doctrine. Wright's view of imputed righteousness is deficient in three areas. First, it is deficient on its forensic premise that God, who is the righteous Judge, rules in favor of his covenant people despite their sinfulness.[10] Second, it is deficient because there is no exchange between the righteousness of Christ and the ungodly.[11] The ungodly

7. Ibid., 119.

8. Wright, *Justification*, 65–66.

9. Ibid., 136.

10. Wright, *What Saint Paul Really Said*, 97–98; Murray, *Redemption*, 122–24.

11. Cf. Luther, *Luther's Works*, 316; Seifrid, "Righteousness Language," 71.

Critical Evaluation

do not receive the full benefits of Christ's righteousness. Third, it is deficient because its emphasis is on ecclesiology rather than soteriology.[12] The ecclesiological emphasis does not deal with the problem of guilt due to sin.

Deficient on Its Forensic Premise

Wright's view of imputed righteousness is deficient on the actual premise of its forensic example. In his forensic premise, God rules in favor of his covenant family despite their sinfulness. God weighs the sinful evidence set before him by his covenant people and rules in their favor based on his covenant faithfulness. God's ruling is not a ruling of right standing before a righteous Judge. Rather, it is a ruling of right standing in the covenant family.

God's covenant people stand before God in a law court setting seeking a favorable judgment based on God's faithfulness to his covenant people. Based on this relationship, God declares his people as being in right standing within the covenant; nothing more or less occurs in this declaration. In the courtroom setting, God is the Judge. Israel, because of her own sinfulness, finds herself in a fallen state (even by her own actions), oppressed by the wicked pagans, and makes a plea to God. God then vindicates Israel from her oppressors.[13] This action of justice, by which God demonstrates his covenant faithfulness to his beloved Israel, is salvific in nature.[14] In Wright's view, God's declarative action is a continuous process and occurs each time

---

12. Wright, *What Saint Paul Really Said*, 119; Sanders, *Paul and Palestinian*, 424, 544; cf. Horton, "Wright Wednesdays . . . Covenant and Eschatology."

13. Wright, *What Saint Paul Really Said*, 98.

14. Wright, *Justification*, 242.

the covenant member makes a plea before God.[15] Further, God's declarative action appears to take a lesser view of the severity of sin committed by the sinner to the point of disregarding it altogether.

In regard to the forensic law court setting, Wright calls the traditional view of God's declaration a "category mistake."[16] What he means by this is that the law court setting would not permit the action prescribed in the tradition view. He states, "it makes no sense whatever to say that the judge imputes, imparts, bequeaths, conveys or otherwise transfers his righteousness."[17] He goes on to say that "Righteousness is not an object, a substance or a gas which can be passed across the courtroom."[18] By describing the traditional view in these terms, Wright distorts the traditional view of imputed righteousness. He also does what he accuses tradition of doing and makes a category mistake. First, he equates and associates the word "imputes" with the words "imparts, bequeaths, conveys or otherwise transfers." The words do not have the same exact meaning. The word *imputes* is a bookkeeping term used in the same vein as the words "credits or reckons." Wright then makes the accusation that tradition mistakenly views God's righteousness as a gas or a substance passed from God to the ungodly.[19] Traditional Protestant Reformed church fathers who helped develop the doctrine of imputed righteousness would never use Wright's analogy to describe this doctrine.

Wright concedes to the traditional view that imputed righteousness is a forensic declaration of righteousness

15. Ibid., 62–63; Wright, *What Saint Paul Really Said*, 96–99.

16. Wright, *Justification*, 232; Wright, *What Saint Paul Really Said*, 98.

17. Wright, *What Saint Paul Really Said*, 98.

18. Ibid.

19. Wilson, "Category Mistake."

Critical Evaluation

made by God. The declaration of righteousness by God in Wright's view is not the same as the traditional view. In the traditional view, God weighs the evidence and delivers a righteous verdict based on truth. It is by his divine truth that God condemns the wicked and justifies the righteous. For the redeemed, those who have through faith received the imputation of the righteousness of Christ, this means justification. For it is not the sinfulness of the redeemed that bears the weight of God's judgment; it is the perfect righteousness of Christ that constitutes God's declarative act of justification credited to the ungodly. Justification occurs when the Judge declares the ungodly sinner righteous by the merit of the law. The declaration of righteousness can only happen through the imputation of a righteousness that does not come from the ungodly sinner. In other words, the Judge simply weighs the evidence and announces his findings. This is not a declaration whereby the Judge *places* the person in *right covenant standing*. Conversely, it is a declaration that places the person righteous before God.[20]

Theologian Henri Blocher finds it difficult to acknowledge evidence to support Wright's view that God's declaration simply means membership into the covenant family.[21] This is to say: God's justification of the ungodly through his declarative action of righteousness is more than just placing the ungodly in right covenant standing. John Murray writes, "[T]he mere notion of declaring to be righteous is seen to be inadequate of itself to express the fullness of what is involved in God's justification of the ungodly."[22] The basic premise of Wright's view of imputed righteousness is that God's declaration of righteousness is a right status pronouncement only and not a membership announcement.

20. Murray, *Redemption*, 122–24.
21. Blocher, "Justification," 499.
22. Murray, *Redemption*, 122.

Deficiencies in the Justification of the Ungodly

In further examining declared righteousness in a forensic setting, Mark Seifrid in his study of righteousness language writes that Paul's use of righteousness language originates in Hebrew Scripture, finding "its basis in creational theology rather than in the framework of covenantal ideas."[23] Righteousness language from creational theology finds its relevance in passages that have to do with the administration of God's divine justice. In other words, righteousness in the Pauline writings finds its basis in creational theology (viz., a new creation), not covenantal theology.

Seifrid further states that the use of God's saving righteousness occurs four times more often than the use of divine righteousness in a punitive justice setting. Divine righteousness in punitive justice entails the wrath of God against sin. God's saving righteousness entails God's justification of the ungodly.[24] Righteousness language, for Paul, pertains to God's justice in a creational theological framework. Therefore, God's declaration of righteousness through the imputation of the righteousness of Christ makes the ungodly a new creation.[25]

For Wright, righteousness language has to do with the covenantal idea, not the justification of the ungodly, which in effect brings about a new creation. Again, Wright contends that "justification is God's declaration that someone is in the right, is a member of the sin-forgiven covenant family, while salvation is the actual rescue from death and sin."[26] This view fails to deal with the justification of the ungodly that comes from the human problem of guilt before God. In other words, although the covenant member is in right covenant standing and Christ's has made atonement for sin,

23. Seifrid, "Paul's Use," 40.
24. Seifrid, "Righteousness Language," 415–16.
25. Seifrid, "Paul's Use, 40.
26. Wright, *Justification*, 170.

Critical Evaluation

the covenant member is still a sinner, albeit forgiven. The pollution of sin remains a problem on the conscience for the covenant member. In Wright's view, there is no allowance for an exchange between the perfect righteousness of Christ and the fallen righteousness of the ungodly.

Deficient for Lack of a Blessed Exchange

The second deficiency in Wright's view of imputed righteousness comes from his denial of an *exchange* between Christ and the ungodly. Wright believes that there is no exchange or imputation between the life and work of Christ unto death and the ungodly. True believers do not receive credit for the righteous and perfectly obedient life unto death lived by Christ to satisfy the sin of humanity against God. The cross is merely a demonstration of the faithfulness of Christ, not a "treasury of merit which can then be 'reckoned' to the believer."[27] Justification comes to God's covenant people through Christ, who deals with the problem of sin on the cross as Israel's true representative.[28] Imputed righteousness, as Holy Scripture describes it, merely refers to a declaration of right standing in the covenant for believers.

In the traditional Reformed view, the imputation of the righteousness of Christ is more than just receiving credit based on Christ's fulfillment of the law. It means conformity with God in the perfect sense. This is impossible for fallen humans to accomplish without an exchange between Christ and the ungodly. Luther refers to this exchanged as the "blessed exchange between Christ and the

27. Ibid., 228.
28. Ibid., 117, 228, 106, 133; Wright, *What Saint Paul Really Said*, 49, 93.

Deficiencies in the Justification of the Ungodly

sinner."[29] Melanchthon uses Aristides[30] the just citizen as an example of worldly justification as opposed to Godly justification. Melanchthon writes, "Aristides is a just citizen, we say, meaning that he does what the laws command, and he does not act contrary to them."[31] Perfect obedience to the law, which is nevertheless impossible for fallen sinners, is still not enough to gain entry into heaven. The ungodly must obtain perfect conformity with God. Therefore, God himself must be, as Melanchthon puts it, "in the saved, and makes them [the ungodly] like himself, so that they are entirely pure, without sin."[32] This is why the ungodly must receive their justification through the righteousness of Christ.

Wright disagrees with this view, and his response to how the ungodly benefit from the life and work of Christ is confusing. The confusion comes in his definition of justification and Christ's role in it. He contends that justification comes to God's covenant people through the faithfulness of Christ. There is no imputation of the righteousness of Christ to the ungodly in a blessed exchange between Christ and humanity.

Wright, to support his argument, references on several occasions *pistis Christou*, which he believes means the *faithfulness of Christ* rather than *faith in Christ*. He opposes the notion of making a subjective–objective genitive mistake when translating the phrase to mean faith in Christ rather

---

29. Seifrid, "Paul's Use," 71.

30. "Aristides," *Columbia Electronic Encyclopedia*. Aristides, also known as Aristides the Just, lived in the fifth century BC. He was a man with an indisputable moral reputation adhering to the highest principles moral and righteous living. He was an Athenian general and statesman, one of ten generals who commanded the Athenian military during the Battle of Marathon. He later became the chief magistrate in Athens.

31. Melanchton, *Christian Doctrine*, 161.

32. Ibid.

Critical Evaluation

than the faithfulness of Christ.³³ The faith of the sinner is not the instrumental basis of salvation but the badge of justification.³⁴ In other words, the faith of sinners has nothing to do with their salvation. Their salvation comes from the faithfulness of Christ unto death. The faith of sinners has to do with their demonstration of membership in God's covenant family. He reiterates that it is not about salvation; it is about status. Faith is not the instrument of justification (i.e., faith in Christ). Justification comes to God's covenant people through the faithfulness of Christ. For God's covenant people, faith is not a matter of salvation from God's wrath but rather the demonstration of covenant status. It is through Christ's faithfulness unto death that salvation comes to God's covenant people. In Wright's explanation, he acknowledges that through Christ's faithful obedience salvation comes to God's covenant family because God through Christ deals with the problem of sin. However, he denies any exchange of the works of Christ to the ungodly. For Wright, it is either the faithfulness *of* Christ or faith *in* Christ, but not both.

The confusion continues because he has written extensively about Christ's faithful obedience as the *substitutionary atonement* for and *true representative* of Israel in God's single plan for the salvation of humanity. His stance on these issues is extremely confusing because it appears to be a contradiction of his final analysis of the traditional doctrine of imputed righteousness.³⁵ The question arises that if Christ is God's atonement for the sins of humanity, how are the benefits of this atonement transferred or conveyed to his covenant people. Wright does not believe that Christ,

33. Wright, *Paul*, 111–12; Wright, *Justification*, 104–5, 151, 203.

34. Wright, *Justification*, 207–9.

35. Ibid., 105–6; Wright, *1 Corinthians*, 202–6; Wright, *2 Corinthians*, 66; Wright, *Romans Part 1*, 135–38.

Deficiencies in the Justification of the Ungodly

the atonement representative of Israel, imputes righteousness to his covenant people.[36] However, God's covenant people are the beneficiaries of the work of Christ. Wright attributes these benefits to *being in Christ* or *in union with Christ* as his covenant people, without giving allowance to an imputation.[37] Wright states, "It is not the 'righteousness' of Jesus Christ which is 'reckoned' to the believer. It is his death and resurrection."[38] This contradiction appears to be a game of semantics whereby Wright's apparent resistance comes from a theological viewpoint grounded in tradition but intertwined in a new perspective belief system.

Wright's NPP view dictates his view on imputed righteousness. As he sees it, God imputes or reckons the ungodly not with Christ's righteousness but rather with the recognition of status in his covenant family, giving the ungodly the right to "share table fellowship"[39] with God. Therefore, God deals with the problem of sin through the faithfulness of Jesus Christ, *pistis Christou*.[40] Part of this statement is theologically correct according to tradition. God does justify the ungodly whereby he places them in covenant and table fellowship; however, it is only through the imputation of the righteousness of Christ that justification occurs. Again, Wright tends to blend traditional theology with his new perspective view, making it difficult to discern his NPP view with that of traditional theology, resulting in confusion for nascent Christians or those Christians not studied in the traditional views. For these Christians, Wright's views in this area of theology gives the

---

36. Horton, "Wright Wednesdays . . . Covenant and Eschatology."

37. Wright, *Climax*, 48; Wright, *Resurrection*, 305; Wright, *Paul*, 116.

38. Wright, *Justification*, 232.

39. Ibid., 116.

40. Ibid., 116–17.

Critical Evaluation

misassumption that Wright makes theological discoveries never before considered by church fathers and theological scholars of the past.

When delving further into God's justification of the ungodly through the exchange of sinfulness and righteousness, Abraham comes to mind. Genesis 15:6 states, "And he [Abraham] believed the Lord; and the Lord reckoned it to him as righteousness." Abraham believes God and his promises. The means by which God imputed righteousness to Abraham is his faith in God. Even in the time of Abraham, salvation by faith alone came through God's declared righteousness.[41] According to Saint Augustine, Abraham's salvation came through faith, not through any works of the law, because God had not yet given the law to Israel. The glory came from God and not through the merit of any works by Abraham's obedience. Punishment as a sinner would be a just wage for Abraham's obedience, rather than righteousness.[42] In other words, Abraham's belief in God's promises indicates that "he had no actual righteousness, but was credited with that which he did not in himself possess."[43]

Although Wright believes that Abraham was an ungodly sinner, Wright does not believe that God counted or reckoned sin against Abraham because of his covenant promise to Abraham. Wright, however, does allow for the imputation of Adam's sin to humanity. By this he means that Adam brought sin into the world and from sin came death to all humanity. He further acknowledges that Israel was in the loins of Adam.[44]

41. Wood, *Survey of Israel's History*, 43.

42. Augustine, *Romans*, 6–9.

43. Dodd, *Romans*, 68.

44. Wright, *Justification*, 99; Wright, *What Saint Paul Really Said*, 33, 130, 140.

Deficiencies in the Justification of the Ungodly

As mentioned before, Wright believes that God deals with the problem of sin through the faithfulness of Jesus Christ, who was obedient, where Israel failed in God's *single-plan-through-Israel-for-the-world*.[45] However, he disagrees that the ungodly receive credit for Christ's faithful obedience through the imputation of righteousness, which brings justification. Therefore, according to Wright, the doctrine of imputed righteousness in a traditional sense is not necessary.

If, according to Wright, there is no exchange between Christ and the ungodly, there is no mechanism in place for dealing with the sinful nature of the ungodly. The problem arises in Wright's view when he fails to show how God, through his divine integrity, justifies the guilt or the feeling of guilt by the forgiven sinner. By Wright's own definition, God declares the covenant member in right standing within the covenant, which is only a forensic declaration that demonstrates God's faithfulness to his covenant people.[46] However, Wright's view does not deal completely with the pollution or corruption of the soul, only the penalty for sin. In other words, the declaration grants forgiveness for sin but the guilty sinful nature remains. Further, it does not deal with God's divine integrity for being just—and that is to punish sinners. God may declare the ungodly righteous but this does not mean that the ungodly are "good, morally upright or virtuous."[47] It merely means that the ungodly receive a favorable ruling from God.

Traditional theologians such as Michael Horton and Thomas Oden agree that God's decree does not make the ungodly good, morally upright, or virtuous; however, they do consider God's declaration of righteousness to the ungodly

45. Wright, *Justification*, 96.
46. Wright, *What Saint Paul Really Said*, 99.
47. Ibid., 98.

Critical Evaluation

a merciful and virtuous act.[48] The reason Wright's view falls short in its dealing with the guilt of the sinner is because there is no forgiveness without perfect righteousness.[49] The law is not relaxed or set aside. Disobedience of God's commands, whether it be Adam's sin[50] or actual sin,[51] brings a sense of shame and guilt (i.e., a guilty conscience).[52] Jesus Christ fulfills the law through his perfect righteousness.[53] The mechanism in place that justifies the ungodly is the imputation of a perfect righteousness from Christ received by the ungodly through faith.

In Wright's view of justification, the struggle for the ungodly is to obtain and maintain covenant membership rather than to deal with the problem of having a sinful nature. His view does not deal with the person's inclination to sin and, after sinning, the feeling of culpability (self-reproach) although forgiven. The prophet Isaiah's encounter with God in Isaiah 6 demonstrates the deficiency in Wright's view. The prophet Isaiah was a part of God's covenant family, in good or "right" standing. He was blameless as to the requirements of the law. Yet, he became undone as he stood before a righteous God.

Righteousness, for Wright, begins by grace but continues through the guidance of the Holy Spirit in the process of sanctification. The state of sanctification carries with

---

48. Horton, "Wright Wednesdays . . . Covenant and Eschatology."

49. Oden, *Justification Reader*, 36–37.

50. Wimmer, "Original Sin," 993. Adam's sin sometimes called *original sin*, a term first used by Saint Augustine. A more accurate description is that Adam's evil action in the garden brought an "evil inclination" and the universality of sin into the world.

51. Morris, "Sin, Guilt," 877–81. Although not the same as Adam, humanity's transgressions against God is sin and also leads to death.

52. Hodge, *Systematic Theology*, 2:123.

53. Oden, *Justification Reader*, 36–37.

Deficiencies in the Justification of the Ungodly

it an obligation in what can amount to a self-justification process.[54] For Wright, it is justification through one's own righteousness, which is inherent not imputed.[55]

Furthermore, Wright's view also rejects the metaphor of the clothing of Christ's righteousness as an illustration for imputed righteousness, although he does make the illustrative connection in his commentary of Philippians 3 of how the Jewish law of Torah clothes Paul in righteousness.[56] To further complicate his view, Wright resists imputation language regarding the righteousness of Christ to the ungodly, despite his belief that Jesus the Messiah fulfills the demands of the law—something that Adam and the nation of Israel failed to do but are now the beneficiaries of this fulfillment.[57]

Deficient per Emphasis on Ecclesiology Rather than Soteriology

The third deficiency in Wright's view of imputed righteousness comes with his emphasis on ecclesiology rather than soteriology. The purpose of this critique is not to set ecclesiology against soteriology. Both biblical doctrines are vital and complimentary to one another in God's renewal of humanity.[58] Rather, the purpose is to examine the deficiency in Wright's view.

According to Wright, God declares the ungodly as being in right standing in the covenant. For Gentile believers,

---

54. Macleod, *Faith to Live By*, 166–67.

55. Ibid.

56. Wright, *Justification*, 145.

57. Horton, "Wright Wednesdays . . . Justification and Romans."

58. Horton, "Wright Wednesdays . . . Soteriology and Ecclesiology."

this is a declaration of church membership with the Jews in God's single family.[59] The deficiency in this view is that it is an ecclesiastical declarative membership emphasis, not a soteriological declarative action by Christ on behalf of the ungodly. Again, it does not deal with the problem of guilt from the sins of the ungodly. It places the ungodly in a right membership status, but does not place them in a right status before God.

Justification, according to Wright, is not about the salvation of the ungodly. He states, "In standard Christian theological language, it wasn't so much about soteriology as about ecclesiology; not so much about salvation as about the church."[60] This view does not deal with a person's righteous standing before God, rather it deals with a person's right standing in relationship to another person.[61]

Wright's view of imputed righteousness fails to justify the sinner because its focus is on a declared status as it pertains to the covenant family rather than a righteous status before God. Therefore, the struggle for the ungodly is to demonstrate covenant membership rather than to affirm the saving work of Jesus Christ received by faith, which is the entry point of salvation.[62]

Faith, in Wright's view, is a badge that exhibits covenant membership.[63] In other words, faith is the badge of covenant status, not the instrument through which the ungodly receive salvation. Justification is about signs that demonstrate membership in God's covenant family.[64] This

---

59. Wright, *Justification*, 99, 112, 116.

60. Wright, *What Saint Paul Really Said*, 119.

61. Horton, "Wright Wednesdays . . . Soteriology and Ecclesiology."

62. Ibid.

63. Wright, *What Saint Paul Really Said*, 129–30.

64. Ibid., 119.

Deficiencies in the Justification of the Ungodly

view does not deal with the problem of sin and the wrath of God in judgment upon this sin, which means eternal damnation. Nor does he deal with the question of how God justifies the unjust. Wright's new perspective view limits him to only addressing the question of who is in right covenant standing by the demonstration of covenant boundary markers.[65]

In defense of his ecclesiological view, Wright describes justification as a rescue operation whereby God comes to a fallen chaotic world and rescues his elect (both Jews and Gentiles). He does not believe that justification is the process by which sinners receive salvation by God's grace for those who believe. Justification is a faith process whereby a person believes and receives salvation through the community of covenant membership.[66]

In Wright's struggle to explain his emphasis on ecclesiology over soteriology, he gives the impression that these two doctrines are in conflict with one another from a traditional viewpoint. But the doctrines of soteriology and ecclesiology, from a traditional view, are not in conflict with each other. Rather, ecclesiology derives from soteriology. The problem, as traditional theologian Douglas Kelly views it, is that Wright has the cart before the horse.[67] Ecclesiology comes from soteriology.

Wright's emphasis on ecclesiology comes from his second temple NPP view, which holds that vindication will come to the nation of Israel and therefore the age to come is their inheritance. However, for this to happen, Israel is to maintain the law "through penitence and amendment of life."[68] Consequently, contemporary Christians must dem-

65. Kelly, "New Approaches."
66. Wright, *Paul*, 121–22.
67. Kelly, "New Approaches."
68. Wright, *Justification*, 76.

Critical Evaluation

onstrate a similar lifestyle of obedience and faith to obtain their inheritance as a part of God's covenant in the eschatological judgment still to come. The works of the law (faith) demonstrate covenant membership and distinguish God's chosen from everyone else.[69]

This view results in Christian believers having a feeling of uncertainty. It echoes the same uncertainty regarding justification as written about in Roman Catholic dogma (viz., the Council of Trent) regarding justification. According to Trent,

> If one considers his own weakness and his defective disposition, he may well be fearful and anxious as to the state of grace, as nobody knows with the certainty of faith, which permits of no error, that he has achieved the grace of God.[70]

The uncertainty comes when trying to determine whether a Christian is living a life that is obedient enough and can maintain this obedience until death or the eschaton. For Wright, faith through the guidance of the Holy Spirit is the badge that demonstrates covenant membership through an obedient life.[71]

According to this view, an obedient life as a covenant member demonstrates justification. However, problems arise when the fear of apostasy for disobedient Christians becomes a focus on legalism and not on Christ. The life may also venture into the area of merit whereby the Christian may gain a feeling of entitlement. H. A. A. Kennedy writes about the problems of legalism in Palestinian Judaism. He states,

---

69. Ibid., 117, 172.
70. Ott, *Fundamentals*, 262; Grudem, *Systematic Theology*, 728.
71. Wright, *Justification*, 185.

Deficiencies in the Justification of the Ungodly

> But as this obedience came to involve the observance of minute regulations, the notion of merit was bound to insinuate itself, as so the rigid contract-conception overshadowed that of Covenant, which rested on the mercy of God.[72]

Living an ecclesiastical life whereby the focus is on maintaining covenant membership also echoes scholar Thomas Aquinas' view of justification. Aquinas asserts that God infuses grace upon a person thereby making that person just. This was the predominate view of the Roman Catholic Church during the Middle Ages, which later developed into a justification system of merit.[73] Although not necessarily intended, the fear is that Wright's view of justification can become a system of merit.

Scripture, from a traditional view, demonstrates otherwise. The struggle for salvation finds its end through justification by imputed righteousness. Horton puts it this way: "The formal cause of our salvation is God's grace, the material cause (or ground) is Christ, and the instrument through which we receive it is faith: salvation by grace, in Christ, through faith."[74] Faith is the instrument because, according to Paul, "faith is reckoned as righteousness" (Rom 4:5).

The struggle for Christians, from Wright's viewpoint, is to determine whether they are in the covenant, albeit

---

72. Kennedy, "Significance and Range," 392; Sanders, *Paul and Palestinian*, 419–20.

73. Berkhof, *Systematic Theology*, 512; cf. Hardon, *Catholic Catechism*, 560–62. In Roman Catholic doctrine a system of merit called indulgences exists whereby payment for the penalty of sins comes through a treasury of merit earned by virtue of the works of Christ and his church (the Blessed Virgin Mary and the saints). An indulgence pays the penalty in lieu of temporal punishment for the remission of sins, and is a extra sacramental revelation of God's justice.

74. Horton, "Wright Wednesdays . . . Covenant and Eschatology."

Critical Evaluation

right covenant standing, rather than having faith in God for justification through the righteousness of Christ imputed to them by faith. The view, where the focus of justification is on ecclesiology rather than soteriology, leaves the Christian seeking to live a life worthy of being able to stay in covenant rather than living a life in response to and reliance on the gospel.

Part of Wright's problem as he defends his new perspective viewpoint on imputed righteousness is that he has the tendency to combine two distinctly recognized biblical doctrines together to form a new view of the doctrine of justification, which poses a problem to Christians. He combines the doctrine of justification with the doctrine of sanctification to form his eschatological justification view. Therefore, sanctification has a direct bearing on whether or not an individual ultimately receives justification.

The combining of both these doctrines is not new in church history. Although the doctrines of justification and sanctification are inseparable, problems arose during the first and second centuries because there was no clear distinction between justification and sanctification, which led to a salvation-by-works mentality.[75]

Church history appears to be repeating itself. The blending of both doctrines is the reason Wright vehemently denies the traditional doctrine of justification, which Martin Luther states is the article by which the church stands or falls. Wright believes that the doctrine of imputed righteousness from a traditional perspective is not necessary. Christians, according to Wright, need only to demonstrate their ecclesiastical membership through their badge of faith by obedience until death or the eschaton in order to demonstrate their justification.[76]

75. Lovelace, *Dynamics*, 99.
76. Wright, *Justification*, 128, 151.

Deficiencies in the Justification of the Ungodly

The traditional view of justification holds that a person stands justified before God based on the redemptive work of Jesus Christ imputed to the ungodly through faith. Sanctification is the expression of living a holy life in Christ.[77] This is the view of Luther, which states that God justifies the ungodly through the imputation of the righteousness of Christ.

The study of Holy Scripture reveals an exclusive rule regarding justification. God only justifies the ungodly.[78] If this is the case, the struggle for the ungodly is not an ecclesiological problem, as Wright believes, but a soteriological problem the resolution of which comes with the imputation of the righteousness of Christ.

EVALUATION

The deficiencies in Wright's view of imputed righteousness stem from the dictates of his NPP viewpoint. In order to support his NPP view, he claims that Christians, like the Jews of the OT, must demonstrate their right covenant standing by faith. This faith is not the means by which Christians respond to the gospel call for salvation, but a display of membership in God's family. It is for this reason that Wright confronts a doctrine, albeit in a deficient manner, calling it a category mistake.

Wright's NPP view of the doctrine of imputed righteous reveals deficiencies in the justification of the ungodly. As aforementioned, these deficiencies come in Wright's view of the forensic declaration whereby God appears to overlook or downplay sin. This view is counter to the biblical message of justice whereby justification comes to the

77. Lovelace, *Dynamics*, 98.
78. Seifrid, *Christ, Our Righteousness*, 68.

Critical Evaluation

righteous and condemnation comes to the wicked (Deut 25:1). A righteous judge must make a righteous ruling (Prov 17:15). If not, the judge is anathema before God.

The deficiencies also include a lack of exchange or imputation between the righteousness of Christ and the ungodly. Sinners do not receive the full benefit of Christ's perfectly obedient life unto death, which brings perfect conformity to God. They are not the beneficiaries of a perfect righteousness that allows them to stand before God justified. Albeit, Wright acknowledges the substitutionary atoning work of Christ for sin, but he denies any imputation of Christ's atoning work to the unrighteous. Without the imputation of the righteousness of Christ, the sinner (although forgiven) maintains a feeling of culpability for his/her sinful actions. This, again, is what the prophet Isaiah experienced when called before the presence of God (Isa 6). Isaiah was a part of the covenant family in right standing. He was blameless as to the requirements of the law. Yet, he pronounced curses upon himself as he stood before a truly righteousness God.

Furthermore, Wright's view is deficient in its emphasis on ecclesiology over soteriology. Justification, for Wright, appears as a work of merit that demonstrates membership through the exhibition of the badge of faith. Justification is not a response to the gospel message; that comes by the power of the Holy Spirit, who regenerates through the means of faith in the work of Christ unto death by the grace of the Father. Justification, according to Wright, is a struggle to demonstrate membership rather than the means by which salvation comes to the ungodly.

The importance of obtaining the correct understanding of justification through the doctrine of imputed righteousness rests on the message of the gospel. In the process of justification, the Holy Spirit regenerates, the ungodly

Deficiencies in the Justification of the Ungodly

respond to the message of the gospel in faith, and God imputes (reckons or credits) this response as righteousness. As with Abraham, the ungodly believe and God imputes this faith as righteousness. The ungodly through the means of faith worship and glorify God.[79]

The call of the gospel is not a call to demonstrate membership; it is a call in the process of salvation through justification. The works of merit in the demonstration of faith do not determine the eschatological destiny of the ungodly. Rather, God determines their eschatological destiny before the foundation of the universe. The action of the ungodly through God's declaration of righteousness transforms them into people who are acceptable in his sight.[80]

---

79. Luther, *Romans*, 71.
80. Morris, *Matthew*, 638–39.

Conclusion

THROUGHOUT THE STORY OF redemption, God's providence reigns even in the midst of human theological intellectual debate, including Wright's new perspective view and the traditional Reformed view of imputed righteousness. The message of the gospel is the power of God for salvation. Despite humanity's best efforts, the basic message of the gospel remains more powerful than the messengers who try to interpret, explain, or deliver it. Justification through the imputation of the righteousness of Christ remains the *articlus stantis et cadentis ecclesiae*, the fundamental article of faith in the church of Jesus Christ.

Challenges to the traditional understanding of justification, particularly the doctrine of imputed righteousness by Wright, revitalize the biblical and theological communities. These challenges provide an opportunity to reexamine and perhaps adjust one's theological view of the Pauline epistles. Although Wright bring a different interpretation to the Pauline writings of the doctrine of imputed righteousness, his interpretation of this doctrine fails to sufficiently deal with the justification of the ungodly. The deficiencies in his view render the call of the gospel message as a status acknowledgement, rather than the process of salvation whereby the ungodly affirm the call by faith. As with

Deficiencies in the Justification of the Ungodly

Abraham, faith is the means by which the ungodly glorify God. God imputes this belief as righteousness.[1] Faith is not the righteousness by which justification comes to the ungodly.[2] The righteousness that justifies is the imputed righteousness of Christ. It is because of Christ's imputed righteousness credited to the ungodly that Christians stand before God justified. This is how an eternally righteous God justifies the ungodly. The story of redemption starts with the trespass of Adam and comes to fruition through the righteousness of Christ.

> If, because of the one man's trespass, death exercised dominion through that one, much more surely will those who receive the abundance of grace and the free gift of righteousness exercise dominion in life through the one man, Jesus Christ. (Rom 5:17)

Justification comes to the ungodly by the grace of God the Father through the imputation of the righteousness of Jesus Christ by the power of the Holy Spirit.

---

1. Morris, *Galatians*, 98–100.
2. Murray, *Redemption*, 125.

Bibliography

Althaus, Paul. *The Theology of Martin Luther*. Philadelphia: Fortress, 1966.

Anderson, Jeff S. *The Internal Diversification of Second Temple Judaism*. New York: University Press of America, 2002.

Anselm. *Why God Became Man and The Virgin Conception and Original Sin*. Translated by Joseph M. Colleran. Albany: Magi, 1969.

"Aristides." *Columbia Electronic Encyclopedia*. 6th ed. Academic Search Complete, EBSCOhost (accessed July 2010).

Athanasius, Saint. "Introduction to Athanasius: Background and Ideas." In *Christology of the Later Fathers,* edited by Edward R. Hardy. Philadelphia: Westminster, 1954.

———. "On the Incarnation of the Word." In *Christology of the Later Fathers,* translated by Archibald Robertson, edited by Edward R. Hardy. Philadelphia: Westminster, 1954.

———. *St. Athanasius on the Incarnation: The Treatise De Incarnatione Verbi Dei*. Crestwood, NY: St. Vladimir's Seminary Press, 1953.

Augustine, Saint. *Augustine on Romans: Propositions from the Epistle to the Romans Unfinished Commentary on the Epistle to the Romans*. Edited by Paula F. Landes. Chico, CA: Scholars, 1982.

———. *Augustine's Commentary on Galatians*. Translated by Eric Plumer. Oxford: Oxford University Press, 2003.

———. "De Natura et Gratia." In *Corpus Scriptorum Ecclesiasticorum Latinorum*, vol. 60, edited by C. F. Urba and J Zycha. Vienna: Tempsky, 1913.

———. "The Spirit and the Letter." In *The Works of St. Augustine: A Translation for the 21st Century*, vol. 23, translated by Roland Teske, edited by John E. Rotelle. New York: Hyde Park, 1997.

Bibliography

Bailey, Sarah P. "N. T. Wright Retiring as Bishop." *Christianity Today*, April 27, 2010. Online: http://blog.christianitytoday.com/ctliveblog/archives/2010/04/n_t_wright_to_r.html.

Barrett, C. K. *The Epistle to the Romans*. New York: Harper, 1957.

Barth, Karl. *The Epistle to the Romans*. Translated by Edwyn C. Hoskyns. 6th ed. New York: Oxford University Press, 1968.

Barth, Markus. *Justification: Pauline Texts Interpreted in the Light of the Old and New Testaments*. Translated by A. M. Woodruff. Grand Rapids: Eerdmans, 1971.

Beeke, Joel R., and Sinclair B. Ferguson, editors. *Reformed Confessions: Harmonized*. Grand Rapids: Baker, 1999.

Berkhof, Louis. *Manual of Christian Doctrine*. Grand Rapids: Eerdmans, 1933.

———. *Systematic Theology*. Grand Rapids: Eerdmans, 1996.

Berkouwer, G. C. *Faith and Justification: Studies in Dogmatics*. Grand Rapids: Eerdmans, 1963.

Bird, Michael F. *The Saving Righteousness of God: Studies on Paul, Justification and the New Perspective*. Milton Keynes, UK: Paternoster, 2007.

Blocher, Henri A. "Justification of the Ungodly (Sola Fide): Theological Reflections." In *Justification and Variegated Nomism: A Fresh Appraisal of Paul and Second Temple Judaism*, edited by D. A. Carson et al., vol. 2, 499. Grand Rapids: Baker Academic, 2004.

Bromily, Geoffrey W. *Theological Dictionary of the New Testament: Abridged in One Volume*, edited by Gerhard Friedrich and Gerhard Kittel. Grand Rapids: Eerdmans, 2000.

Bultmann, Rudolf. *Theology of the New Testament*. Translated by Kendrick Grobel. New York: Scribner's, 1951.

Cadbury, Henry J. *The Peril of Modernizing Jesus*. London: Macmillan, 1937.

Calvin, John. *Commentaries on the Epistles of Paul the Apostle to the Philippians, Colossians, and Thessalonians*, edited and translated by John Pringle. Edinburgh: Printer to Her Majesty, 1850.

———. *Commentaries on the Epistle of Paul the Apostle to the Romans*. Edited by Henry Beveridge, translated by Christopher Fetherstone. Vol. 2. Grand Rapids: Baker, 2005.

———. "The Mode of Obtaining the Grace of Christ: The Benefits It Confers, and the Effects Resulting from It." In *Institutes of The Christian Religion*, translated by Henry Beveridge, 38. Grand Rapids: Eerdmans, 1989

Calvin, John, and Jacopo Sadoleto. *A Reformation Debate: Sadoleto's Letter to the Genevans and Calvin's Reply with an Appendix on*

Bibliography

the Justification Controversy. Edited by John C. Olin. New York: Harper, 1966.

Carlson, Charles P. *Justification in Earlier Medieval Theology*. The Hague: Nijhoff, 1975.

Carson, D. A. "Mystery and Fulfillment: Toward a More Comprehensive Paradigm of Paul's Understanding of the Old and the New." In *Justification and Variegated Nomism*, edited by D. A. Carson et al., vol. 2, 393. Grand Rapids: Baker Academic, 2004.

———. "Summaries and Conclusions." In *Justification and Variegated Nomism*, edited by D. A. Carson et al., vol. 1, 505. Grand Rapids: Baker Academic, 2001.

———. "The Vindication of Imputation: On Fields of Discourse and Semantic Fields." In *Justification: What's at Stake in the Current Debates*, edited by Mark Husbands et al. Downers Grove, IL: InterVarsity, 2004.

Chance, J. Bradley. "Christian." *Eerdmans Dictionary of the Bible*, edited by David Noel Freedman. Grand Rapids: Eerdmans, 2000.

Chemnitz, Martin. *Justification: The Chief Article of Christian Doctrine as Expounded in Loci Theologici*, edited by Delpha H. Preus, translated by J. A. O. Preus. St. Louis: Concordia, 1985.

Cox, David. *Jung and St. Paul: A Study of the Doctrine of Justification by Faith and Its Relation to the Concept of Individuation*. New York: Association, 1959.

Davies, W. D. *Jewish and Pauline Studies*. Philadelphia: Fortress, 1984.

———. *Paul and Rabbinic Judaism: Some Rabbinic Elements in Pauline Theology*. New York: Harper, 1948.

Davies, W. D., and E. P. Sanders. "Jesus: From the Jewish Point of View." In *The Cambridge History of Judaism: The Early Roman Period*, edited by W. D. Davies, William Horbury, and John Sturdy. Cambridge: Cambridge University Press, 2001.

Dodd, C. H. *The Epistle of Paul to the Romans*. New York: Harper, 1932.

"Duke Religion Professor E. P. Sanders Honored with New Books." *Duke Today, January 6, 2009. Online: http://www.dukenews.duke.edu/2009/01/sanders.html*.

Duncan, J. Ligon, III. "The Attractions of the New Perspective(s) on Paul: A Transcript of a Paper Given in Jackson, Mississippi and Glasgow, Scotland." *Alliance of Confessing Evangelicals*, November 2003. Online: http://www.alliancenet.org/partner/Article_Display_Page/0,,PTID307086_CHID560462_CIID1660662,00.html."

Bibliography

———. "More Concerns about N. T. Wright and the New Perspective(s)." *PCA News*, 2009. Online: http://www.monergism.com/thethreshold/articles/onsite/concerns.html.

Dunn, James D. G. *The Epistle to the Galatians*. Black's New Testament Commentary. London: Hendrickson, 1993.

———. *Jews and Christians: The Parting of the Ways; A.D. 70 to 135*. Grand Rapids: Eerdmans, 1999.

———. *The New Perspective on Paul*. Grand Rapids: Eerdmans, 2005.

———. *The Theology of Paul the Apostle*. Grand Rapids: Eerdmans, 1998.

———. *Unity and Diversity in the New Testament: An Inquiry Into the Character of Earliest Christianity*. Philadelphia: Westminster, 1977.

Elwell, Walter A., and Robert W. Yarbrough. *Encountering the New Testament: A Historical and Theological Survey*. 2nd ed. Grand Rapids: Baker Academic, 2005.

Erickson, Millard J. *Christian Theology*. Grand Rapids: Baker, 1985.

———. *Introducing Christian Doctrine*. Edited by L. Arnold Hustad. 2nd ed. Grand Rapids: Baker Academic, 2004.

Gager, John G. *Reinventing Paul*. New York: Oxford University Press, 2000.

Garlington, Don. "Imputation or Union with Christ?: A Response to John Piper." *Reformation & Revival Journal* 12/4 (Fall 2003) 45–113.

———. "A Study of Justification by Faith." *Reformation & Revival Journal* 11/2 (Spring 2002) 55–73.

Gathercole, Simon. "The Doctrine of Justification in Paul and Beyond: Some Proposals." In *Justification in Perspective: Historical Developments and Contemporary Challenges*, edited by Bruce L. McCormack. Grand Rapids: Baker Academic, 2006.

Geisler, Norman L. *Christian Ethics*. Grand Rapids: Baker, 1989.

Gonzalez, Justo L. *The Story of Christianity*. 2 vols. San Francisco: Harper, 1985.

Grenz, Stanley J. "Jesus as the Imago Dei: Image-of-God Christology and the Non-Linear Linearity of Theology." *Journal of the Evangelical Theological Society* 47/4 (December 2004) 617–628.

Grudem, Wayne. *Systematic Theology: An Introduction to Biblical Doctrine*. Grand Rapids: Zondervan, 1994.

Gundry, Robert H. "The Nonimputation of Christ's Righteousness." In *Justification: What's at Stake in the Current Debates*, edited by Mark Husbands and Daniel J. Treier. Downers Grove, IL: InterVarsity, 2004.

Bibliography

Hardon, John A. *The Catholic Catechism: A Contemporary Catechism of the Teachings of the Catholic Church.* Garden City, NY: Doubleday, 1975.

Heckel, Matthew C. "Is R. C. Sproul Wrong about Martin Luther? An Analysis of R. C. Sproul's Faith Alone: The Evangelical Doctrine of Justification with Respect to Augustine, Luther, Calvin, and Catholic Luther Scholarship." *Journal of the Evangelical Theological Society* 47/1 (March 2004) 89–120.

The Heidelberg Catechism. Grand Rapids: Faith Alive Christian Resources, 1988.

Hill, Charles E. "N. T. Wright on Justification." *RPM Magazine* 3/22 (May 28, 2001). Online: http://thirdmill.org/files/english/new_testament/11926~5_28_01_10-55-11_AM~NT.Hill.Wright.pdf.

Hodge, Charles. *A Commentary on the Epistle to the Ephesians.* Grand Rapids: Eerdmans, 1966.

———. *A Commentary on the Epistle to the Romans.* Grand Rapids: Eerdmans, 1951.

———. *Systematic Theology.* 3 vols. Grand Rapids: Eerdmans, 1965–70.

Hoekema, Anthony A. *Created in God's Image.* Grand Rapids: Eerdmans, 1986.

———. *Saved By Grace.* Grand Rapids: Eerdmans, 1989.

Horne, Mark. "Getting Some Perspective on the New Perspective." *Theologia*, 2002. Online: http://www.hornes.org/theologia/mark-horne/perspective-on-the-new-perspective.

Horton, Michael. "What's All the Fuss About?: The Status of the Justification Debate." *Modern Reformation* 11/2 (March–April 2002) 17–21.

———. "Wright Wednesdays: Part 5. Justification and God's Righteousness: Covenant and Eschatology." *Out of the Horse's Mouth*, September 16, 2009. Online: http://www.whitehorseinn.org/archives/112.html.

———. "Wright Wednesdays: Part 8. Justification and Romans." *Out of the Horse's Mouth*, October 7, 2009. Online: http://www.whitehorseinn.org/archives/151.html.

———. "Wright Wednesdays: Part 9. 'Works of the Law': Soteriology and Ecclesiology." *Out of the Horse's Mouth*, October 21, 2009. Online: http://www.whitehorseinn.org/archives/164.html.

Jones, Ken. "Justification and Sanctification Distinguished." *Modern Reformation* 11/2 (March/April 2002) 29–31.

Bibliography

Joyner, Will. "Krister Stendahl, 1921–2008." Harvard Divinity School News and Events, October 8, 2008. Online: http://www.hds.harvard.edu/news/article_archive/stendahl.html.

Jung, Carl Gustav. *Two Essays on Analytical Psychology*. 2nd ed. Translated by R. F. C. Hull. London: Routledge & Kegan Paul, 1953.

"Jung, Carl Gustav." *Columbia Electronic Encyclopedia*. 6th ed. Academic Search Complete, EBSCOhost (accessed April 29, 2013).

Käsemann, Ernst. *Commentary on Romans*. Translated by Geoffrey W. Bromiley. Grand Rapids: Eerdmans, 1980.

Kelly, Douglas. "New Approaches of Biblical Theology to Justification." *PCA News*, 2009. Online: http://www.alliancenet.org/CC/article/0,,PTID23682_CHID125467_CIID1521174,00.html.

Kennedy, H. A. A. "The Significance and Range of the Covenant-Conception in the New Testament." *Expositor* 10 (1915) 385–410.

Kostlin, Julius. *The Theology of Luther: In Its Historical Development and Inner Harmony*. Translated by Charles E. Hay. Vol. 1. Philadelphia: Lutheran Publication Society, 1897.

Kugel, James L. *The Bible as It Was*. Cambridge, MA: Harvard University Press, 1997.

Kugler, Robert A. "Testaments." In *Justification and Variegated Nomism: The Complexities of Second Temple Judaism*, edited by D. A. Carson, Peter T. O'Brien and Mark A. Seifrid, vol. 1. Grand Rapids: Baker Academic, 2001.

Lovelace, Richard F. *Dynamics of Spiritual Life: An Evangelical Theology of Renewal*. Downers Grove, IL: IVP Academic, 1979.

Luther, Martin. *Bondage of the Will*. Translated by O. R. Johnston and J. I. Packer. Grand Rapids: Revell, 2003.

———. *The Christian Liberty*, edited by Harold J. Grimm. Philadelphia: Fortress, 1957.

———. *A Commentary on the Epistle to the Romans*. Translated by J. Theodore Mueller. Grand Rapids: Zondervan, 1960.

———. *A Commentary on St. Paul's Epistle to the Galatians*. Translated by Theodore Graebner. 4th ed. Grand Rapids: Zondervan, 1953.

———. *Luther's Works: Sermons I*. Edited by John W. Doberstein and Helmut T. Lehmann. Philadelphia: Fortress, 1999.

Macleod, Donald. *A Faith to Live By: Understanding Christian Doctrine*. Scotland: Mentor, 2002.

———. *The Person of Christ: Contours of Christian Theology*. Edited by Gerald Bray. Downers Grove, IL: InterVarsity, 1998.

Bibliography

Matthews, Victor H. "Law." *Eerdmans Dictionary of the Bible*. Grand Rapids: Eerdmans, 2000.

Mattison, Mark M. "Introduction and Summary: The New Perspective on Paul." The Paul Page, December 17, 2007. Online: http://www.thepaulpage.com.

McCormack, Bruce L. "*Justitia Aliena*: Karl Barth in Conversation with the Evangelical Doctrine of Imputed Righteousness." In *Justification in Perspective: Historical Developments and Contemporary Challenges*, edited by Bruce L. McCormack. Grand Rapids: Baker Academic, 2006.

McGrath, Alister E. *Historical Theology: An Introduction to the History of Christian Thought*. Malden, MA: Blackwell, 1998.

———. *Iustitia Dei: A History of the Christian Doctrine of Justification*. 2 vols. New York: Cambridge University Press, 1994.

———. "Justification." *Dictionary of Paul and His Letters*. Downers Grove, IL: InterVarsity, 1993.

———. *A Life of John Calvin: A Study in the Shaping of Western Culture*. Malden, MA: Blackwell, 1990.

———. *Luther's Theology of the Cross: Martin Luther's Theological Breakthrough*. Malden, MA: Blackwell, 1990.

Meeks, Fred E. *Christian Theology: A Survey of Basic Beliefs*. Plainview, TX: Wayland Baptist University, 2006.

Melanchthon, Philip. *Melanchthon and Bucer: The Library of Christian Classics*. Edited by Wilhelm Pauck, translated by Lowell J. Satre. Philadelphia: Westminster, 1969.

———. *Melanchthon on Christian Doctrine: Loci Communes 1555*. Edited by Clyde Manschreck, translated by Clyde Manschreck. Grand Rapids: Baker, 1965.

Mitton, C. Leslie. "Romans VII Reconsidered—I." *Expository Times* 65/3 (December 1953) 78–81.

———. "Romans VII Reconsidered—II." *Expository Times* 65/4 (January 1954) 99–103.

———. "Romans VII Reconsidered—III." *Expository Times* 65/5 (February 1954) 132–35.

Morris, Leon. *The Apostolic Preaching of the Cross*. Grand Rapids: Eerdmans, 1965.

———. *The Atonement: Its Meaning and Significance*. Downers Grove, IL: InterVarsity, 1983.

———. *The Cross in the New Testament*. Grand Rapids: Eerdmans, 1965.

———. *The Epistle to the Romans*. Grand Rapids: Eerdmans, 1988.

Bibliography

———. *Galatians: Paul's Charter of Christian Freedom*. Downers Grove, IL: InterVarsity, 1996.

———. *The Gospel According to Matthew*. Grand Rapids: Eerdmans, 1992.

———. *New Testament Theology*. Grand Rapids: Zondervan, 1990.

———. "Sin, Guilt." *Dictionary of Paul and His Letters*, edited by Gerald F. Hawthorne and Ralph P. Martin. Downers Grove, IL: InterVarsity, 1993.

Mounce, William D. *Basics of Biblical Greek: Grammar*. Grand Rapids: Zondervan, 2003.

Murray, John. *The Epistle to the Romans*. Grand Rapids: Eerdmans, 1997.

———. *The Imputation of Adam's Sin*. Phillipsburg: Presbyterian and Reformed, 1959.

———. *Principles of Conduct*. Grand Rapids: Eerdmans, 1957.

———. *Redemption: Accomplished and Applied*. Grand Rapids: Eerdmans, 1955.

Oden, Thomas C. *The Justification Reader*. Grand Rapids: Eerdmans, 2002.

Ott, Ludwig. *Fundamentals of Catholic Dogma: A One-Volume Encyclopedia of Doctrines of the Catholic Church*. Edited by James C. Bastible, translated by Patrick Lynch. 4th ed. Rockford, IL: Tan Books, 1974.

Packer, J. I. *Concise Theology: A Guide to Historic Christian Beliefs*. Carol Stream, IL: Tyndale House, 1993.

———. "Justification." *New Bible Dictionary*. London: InterVarsity, 1962.

———. *Knowing God*. Downers Grove, IL: InterVarsity, 1973.

Pink, Arthur W. *The Attributes of God*. Blacksburg, VA: Wilder, 2008.

Piper, John. *Counted Righteous in Christ: Should We Abandon the Imputation of Christ's Rigteousness?*. Wheaton, IL: Crossway, 2002.

———. *The Justification of God: An Exegetical & Theological Study of Romans 9:1–23*. 2nd ed. Grand Rapids: Baker, 1993.

———. "A Response to Don Garlington on Imputation." Edited by John H. Armstrong. *Reformation & Revival Journal* 12/4 (Fall 2003) 121–28.

Riddlebarger, Kim. "Reformed Confessionalism and the New Perspective on Paul: A New Challenge to a Fundamental Article of Faith." Online: http://kimriddlebarger.squarespace.com/theological-essays/New%20Perspective%20on%20Paul%20revised%202006.pdf.

Bibliography

Ritschl, Albrecht. *The Christian Doctrine of Justification and Reconciliation: The Positive Development of the Doctrine*. Edited by A. B. Macaulay and H. R. Mackintosh. Eugene, OR: Wipf & Stock, 2004.

Sanders, E. P. *Jesus and Judaism*. Philadelphia: Fortress, 1985.

———. *Paul*. New York: Oxford University Press, 1991.

———. *Paul and Palestinian Judaism: A Comparison of Patterns of Religion*. Philadelphia: Fortress, 1977.

———. *Paul, the Law, and the Jewish Paul*. Philadelphia: Fortress, 1983.

"Duke Religion Professor E.P. Sanders Honored with New Books." *Duke Today*, January 6, 2009.

Scheck, Thomas P. *Origen and the History of Justification: The Legacy of Origen's Commentary on Romans*. Notre Dame: University of Notre Dame Press, 2008.

Schoeps, H. J. *Paul: The Theology of the Apostle in the Light of Jewish Religious History*. Translated by Harold Knight. Philadelphia: Westminster, 1961.

Schreiner, Thomas. R. *Paul, Apostle of God's Glory in Christ: A Pauline Theology*. Downers Grove, IL: InterVarsity, 2001.

Schweitzer, Albert. *The Mysticism of Paul the Apostle*. Translated by William Montgomery. Baltimore: Johns Hopkins University Press, 1998.

Seifrid, Mark A. *Christ, Our Righteousness: Paul's Theology of Justification*, Edited by D. A. Carson. Downers Grove, IL: InterVarsity, 2000.

———. "Luther, Melanchthon and Paul on the Question of Imputation: Recommendations on a Current Debate." In *Justification: What's at Stake in the Current Debates*, edited by Mark Husbands and Daniel J. Treier. Downers Grove, IL: InterVarsity, 2004.

———. "Paul's Use of Righteousness Language against Its Hellenistic Background." In *Justification and Variegated Nomism*, edited by D. A. Carson et al, vol. 2. Grand Rapids: Baker Academic, 2004.

———. "Righteousness Language in the Hebrew Scriptures and Early Judaism." In *Justification and Variegated Nomism*, edited by D. A. Carson et al., vol. 1. Grand Rapids: Baker Academic, 2001.

Silva, Moisés. *Interpreting Galatians: Explorations in Exegetical Method*. 2nd ed. Grand Rapids: Baker Academic, 2001.

"Staff Profile: Professor James D. G. Dunn." Durham University, Department of Theology and Religion. Online: http://www.dur.ac.uk/theology.religion/staff/.

Bibliography

Stanton, Graham N. "Paul's Gospel." In *The Cambridge Companion to St. Paul*, edited by James D. G. Dunn. New York: Cambridge University Press, 2003.

Stendahl, Krister. *Final Account: Paul's Letter to the Romans*. Minneapolis: Fortress, 1995.

———. "Judaism and Christianity: Then and Now." *Harvard Divinity Bulletin* 28/1 (October 1963) 1–9.

———. *Paul among Jews and Gentiles, and Others Essays*. Philadelphia: Fortress, 1976.

———. *The Scrolls and the New Testament*. New York: Harper, 1957.

Thielman, Frank. "Law." *Dictionary of Paul and His Letters*, edited by Gerald F. Hawthorne and Ralph P. Martin, 793–95. Downers Grove, IL: InterVarsity, 1993.

Tuttiett, Laurence. "O Grant Us Light." In *The Hymnal, #284*. Presbyterian Church in the USA, 1895. Online: http://www.hymnary.org/text/o_grant_us_light_that_we_may_know?text=1&textDefault=editor&tab=about&visited=true.

VanLandingham, Chris. *Judgment & Justification in Early Judaism and the Apostle Paul*. Peabody, MA: Hendrickson, 2006.

Venema, Cornelis P. "Evaluating the New Perspective on Paul (5): Works of the Law Human Inability and Boasting." *The Outlook*, November 2003. Online: http://www.reformedfellowship.net/outlook/2003novemberoutlook.pdf.

———. "What Did Saint Paul Really Say?: N. T Wright and the New Perspective(s) on Paul." In *Faith Alone: Answering the Challenges to the Doctrine of Justification*, edited by Gary L. W. Johnson and Guy Prentiss Waters. Wheaton, IL: Crossway, 2006.

Wallace, Daniel B. "Righteousness of God and N. T. Wright." Bible.org, October 2009. Online: http://bible.org/article/δικαιοσύνη-θεοῦ-and-n-t-wright.

Warfield, Benjamin B. *Studies in Theology*. New York: Oxford University Press, 1932.

Waters, Guy Prentiss. *The Federal Vision and Covenant Theology: A Comparative Analysis*. Phillipsburg: P&R, 2006.

———. *Justification and the New Perspective on Paul: A Review and Response*. Phillipsburg: P&R, 2004.

Westerholm, Stephen. "The New Perspective at Twenty-Five." In *Justification and Variegated Nomism: A Fresh Appraisal of Paul and Second Temple Judaism*, edited by D. A. Carson et al., vol. 2. Grand Rapids: Baker Academic, 2004.

Bibliography

Westminster Confession of Faith and Catechisms. Lawrenceville: Christian Education & Publications Committee of the Presbyterian Church in America, 2007.

Williams, Michael D. *Far as the Curse if Found: The Covenant Story of Redemption.* Phillipsburg: P&R, 2005.

Williamson, G. I. *The Westminster Confession of Faith: For Study Classes.* 2nd ed. Phillipsburg: P&R, 2004.

Wilson, Douglas. "A Category Mistake." April 1, 2005. Online: http://www.dougwils.com/N.T.-Wrights-and-Wrongs/A-Category-Mistake.html.

Wimmer, Joseph F. "Original Sin." *Eerdmans Dictionary of the Bible*, edited by David N. Freedman. Grand Rapids: Eerdmans, 2000.

Wood, Leon J. *A Survey of Israel's History.* Grand Rapids: Academic, 1986.

Wright, N. T. *After You Believe: Why Christian Character Matters.* New York: HarperCollins, 2010.

———. *The Challenge of Jesus: Rediscovering Who Jesus Was and Is.* Downers Grove, IL: InterVasity, 1999.

———. *The Climax of the Covenant: Christ and the Law in Pauline Theology.* Minneapolis: Fortress, 1991.

———. *Evil and the Justice of God.* Downers Grove, IL: InterVarsity, 2006.

———. *Justification: God's Plan & Paul's Vision.* Downers Grove, IL: IVP Academic, 2009.

———. "Justification: The Biblical Basis and Its Relevance for Contemporary Evangelism." Excerpt from *The Great Acquittal: Justification by Faith and Current Christian Thought*, edited by Gavin Reid. London: Collins, 1980. Online: http://www.ntwrightpage.com/Wright_Justification_Biblical_Basis.pdf.

———. *The Last Word: Beyond the Bible Wars to a New Understanding of the Authority of Scripture.* New York: HarperCollins, 2005.

———. *Mark for Everyone.* Louisville: Westminster John Knox, 2004.

———. "New Perspective on Paul." In *Justification in Perspective: Historical Developments and Contemporary* Challenges, edited by Bruce L. McCormack. Grand Rapids: Baker Academic, 2006.

———. "New Perspective on Paul." Lecture delivered at the 10th Edinburgh Dogmatics Conference, August 25–28, 2003, Rutherford House, Edinburgh. Online: http://www.ntwrightpage.com/Wright_New_Perspectives.htm.

———. "Paul and Caesar: A New Reading of Romans." In *A Royal Priesthood: The Use of the Bible Ethically and Politically*, edited by C. Bartholomew, 173–93. Carlisle: Paternoster, 2002. Online:

Bibliography

http://www.ntwrightpage.com/Wright_Paul_Caesar_Romans.htm.

———. *Paul for Everyone: 1 Corinthians*. Louisville: Westminster John Knox, 2004.

———. *Paul for Everyone: 2 Corinthians*. Louisville: Westminster John Knox, 2004.

———. *Paul for Everyone: Romans Part 1: Chapters 1–8*. Louisville: Westminster John Knox, 2004.

———. *Paul for Everyone: Romans Part 2: Chapters 9–16*. Louisville: Westminster John Knox, 2004.

———. *Paul for Everyone: The Prison Letters*. Louisville: Westminster John Knox, 2004.

———. *Paul: In Fresh Perspective*. Minneapolis: Fortress, 2005.

———. "Paul in Different Perspectives." Lecture delivered January 3, 2005, Auburn Avenue Presbyterian Church, Monroe, Louisiana. Online: http://www.ntwrightpage.com/Wright_Auburn_Paul.htm.

———. "The Paul of History and the Paul of Faith." *Tyndale Bulletin* 29 (January 1978) 61–88.

———. *The Resurrection of the Son of God*. Vol. 3 of *Christian Origins and the Question of God*. Minneapolis: Fortress, 2003.

———. "Romans and the Theology of Paul." In Pauline Theology, edited by David M. Hay & E. Elizabeth Johnson, 3:30–67. Minneapolis: Fortress, 1995. Online: http://www.ntwrightpage.com/Wright_Romans_Theology_Paul.pdf.

———. "The Shape of Justification." The Paul Page, October 16, 2009. Online: http://www.thepaulpage.com/the-shape-of-justification.

———. *Surprised by Hope: Rethinking Heaven, the Resurrection, and the Mission of the Church*. New York: HarperCollins, 2008.

———. *What Saint Paul Really Said: Was Paul of Tarsus the Real Founder of Christianity?*. Grand Rapids: Eerdmans, 1997.

Wubbenhorst, Karla. "Calvin's Doctrine of Justification: Variations on a Lutheran Theme." In *Justification in Perspective: Historical Developments and Contemporary Challenges*, edited by Bruce L. McCormackS. Grand Rapids: Baker Academic, 2006.

www.ingramcontent.com/pod-product-compliance
Lightning Source LLC
Chambersburg PA
CBHW070929160426
43193CB00011B/1621